Pearls

WISDOM AND ADVICE FROM EMERGING WOMEN LEADERS

Compiled by

SHARVETTE MITCHELL

Pearls: Wisdom and Advice from Emerging Women Leaders

Scriptures marked KJV are taken from the KING JAMES VERSION (KJV): KING JAMES VERSION, public domain.

The Holy Bible, English Standard Version® (ESV®) Copyright © 2001 by Crossway, a publishing ministry of Good News Publishers. All rights reserved. ESV Text Edition: 2016

Scripture taken from the New King James Version®. Copyright © 1982 by Thomas Nelson. Used by permission. All rights reserved.

Scripture quotations marked (NIV) are taken from the Holy Bible, New International Version®, NIV®. Copyright © 1973, 1978, 1984, 2011 by Biblica, Inc.™ Used by permission of Zondervan. All rights reserved worldwide. zondervan.com.

Published by:
Mitchell Productions, LLC
www.Mitchell-Productions.com

Anthology Editor
Chandra Sparks Splond, M.S.E.
www.chandrasparkssplond.com

Book Creation and Design
DHBonner Virtual Solutions, LLC
www.dhbonner.net

Photographer
Kimie James Photography
www.IYQphotography.com

ISBN for print version: 978-1-7333754-6-7
ISBN for hardcover version: 978-1-7333754-8-1
ISBN for eBook version: 978-1-7333754-7-4

Printed in the United States of America

Dedicated to my past, current, and future
Platform Builder clients who allow me to come
alongside them in this journey of business and life.

You are all true jewels and you have poured into me
just as much as I have poured into you.

To God... who has never slacked
on His promises to me.

Table of Contents

Introduction vii

Some People Never Arrive: Embracing Your Unique Gifts 1
DR. TAMARA WILKERSON DIAS

Black Pearl 11
SPRING C JACKSON

Riding the Waves of Wellness 21
PENNY MCPHERSON

You can be Dynamic Despite Dysfunction 33
KATHERINE L. STATEN

The Pearls my Family Left 47
ERIKA BROOKS

Stepping Up and Stepping Out of Your Comfort Zone 57
VALARIE HARRIS

You're Worth the Investment 69
PATRICIA DYER

Diamonds from Pearls 81
NATALIE BRYAN

The Death of Cinderella: Let's Sort the Situation Out 89
LTOMAY DOUGLAS VARLACK-BUTLER

Beautiful, Brilliant, and Broken 103
CARMEN JIMENEZ-PRIDE

Positioning, Visibility, and Authority 109
SHARVETTE MITCHELL

Introduction

Did you know that there are different types, sizes, colors, and surface qualities of pearls? According to Gemological Institute of America (GIA), the world's foremost authority on diamonds, colored stones, and pearls, there are natural pearls and cultured pearls. Natural pearls form in the bodies or mantle tissue of certain mollusks, usually around a microscopic irritant and always without human help of any kind.

The growth of cultured pearls requires human intervention and care, and there are four types of cultured pearls: Akoya, South Sea, Tahitian, and Freshwater. GIA goes on to share that the most familiar colors are white and cream (a light yellowish brown). Black, gray, and silver are also fairly common, but the palette of pearl colors extends to every hue. The main color—or body color—is often modified by additional colors called overtones, which are typically pink, green, purple, or blue. Some pearls also show the iridescent phenomenon known as orient.

Oh, and we can't forget to talk about the various prices of pearls. The value of a pearl can vary dramatically depending on many factors, but a real pearl necklace can cost anywhere from $150 to $10,000-plus. You will see prices higher than that with luxury lines such as Tiffany & Co. with prices between $29,000 and $45,000.

My hope as the visionary author of *Pearls* is that this book, which will read like a collection of short stories, essays, and advice columns, will allow you to walk away with many pearls of wisdom. The chapters are written from various perspectives and life experiences just as varied as the colors, sizes, and prices of pearls, but all holding their own value and weight.

Sharvette Mitchell, Visionary Author of Pearls

Some People Never Arrive: Embracing Your Unique Gifts

DR. TAMARA WILKERSON DIAS

What comes to mind for you when you hear the word *authenticity*?

Authenticity is defined by *Merriam Webster* as true to one's own personality, spirit, or character. For me, I immediately think of the words *honest, real,* and *true.* I think of gorgeous designer bags by Chanel and Louis Vuitton that must be verified through an "authenticity test" to prove they are products of the brands and not knock-off versions.

I also think about people I've worked with who represent authenticity in their work, relationships, and personal journeys. When I think about people who are authentic in my life, they show up unapologetically and aren't afraid to bring their whole selves into any space they're in. They bring their expertise, backgrounds, experiences, and skills and ditch the concern of what everyone else is thinking. In fact, some of the most successful business owners and corporate leaders I know are people who tap into their personal skills and look for opportunities to display them. Not only does their authenticity allow them to shine wherever they are, but it makes the people around them also feel a sense of honesty and openness.

What does authenticity look like for you? Do you wish you could be more authentic? Do you feel like you must become another person when you get to work? You're not alone. In my research, I found a study done by the Institute for Inclusive Leadership that showed that while ninety percent of leaders felt that authenticity at work was important, only seventy percent of them showed up authentically in the workplace. That means that there's thirty percent of people who wish they could be their true selves, but struggle to actually step into who they are. Of the seventy percent who felt they were authentic in the workplace, they felt happier and more fulfilled there. They also felt more engaged and satisfied showing up each day. Imagine if we all could be more authentic and lead happier, more fulfilled, and satisfied lives?

So many people believe in the importance of being real, honest, and open, but so many of us struggle to actually be authentic.

For years in my own journey in leadership, I struggled with what authenticity looked like for me. Much of this had to do with the fact that I took my first leadership position at age twenty-four. Not only was I trying to figure out who I was as a brand-new leader, but I was tasked with leading people who were the same age as my parents and grandparents (and often reminded me that because they were older, they knew best). I found myself constantly questioning if I belonged in my role, and when I wasn't questioning myself, I felt like I had to prove I was "good enough" to lead others.

My days felt like this dance between who I was and who I thought I needed to be, while I longed for the evenings when I could "clock out" and be myself. I wanted to show up without apology. I wanted to come into my workspace and own my role with power and authority.

But I also felt like people were watching me. I didn't know how honest or how open I could be in this position because I knew there were people watching me. I had supporters who were energized to work with me and champion my vision for the organization I was leading. I also had adversaries who believed there was someone else who was a better fit for the role, and they watched me to see when I would fail. I was so focused on both groups that I struggled to gain my footing. I looked at other leaders around me and tried to mimic their leadership style. I read books on leadership, and instead of applying the principles to my existing skills, I ignored who I was to fit into the book's examples. This ultimately led to frustration, cycles of doubt and fear, and an overwhelming sense of dread toward my leadership position.

I needed to embrace my natural talents. I needed to be proud of my skills. I needed to realize that even though I was a young, new leader, I had purpose.

One of my favorite actresses is Viola Davis. I am always fascinated by her ability to translate the deep, meaningful emotions of her characters to those of us in the audience. Anytime I watch her, I am transported into the space of the role she is portraying. If she's happy, I want to rejoice with her. If she's sad, I find myself reaching for my own tissues to cry with her. But, many people don't know that she didn't achieve the height of her film success until she was in her mid-forties. Though she'd been on Broadway and received acclaim for her work in theater, it wasn't until she landed a role in the film *The Help* that people were able to see her talent shine on the big screen. Since then, she's won numerous awards and even dominated on primetime television.

In the midst of my own leadership challenges, I found myself watching an Access Hollywood interview with Davis as she released a new film. A reporter on the red carpet asked her to talk about her reflections on how she stifled her own voice and growth. The reporter acknowledged how accomplished Davis had been and wanted to know how she was able to move beyond blocking her own growth.

Davis replied, "I think that finding your authenticity and being brave enough to step outside and being who you are…you have to fight other people's opinions of who you are. That's just what the journey is. I'm just glad I arrived here. Some people never arrive."

That quote hit me like a ton of bricks.

Some people never arrive. Was I one of those people? If I was, I didn't want to be anymore.

Can you imagine going your entire life thinking that you aren't good enough? Spending your time obsessing over the qualities that everyone else has? Wasting days because the gifts you have aren't the gifts you want? This was my narrative for those first couple of years in my leadership journey. I battled the internal weight of wanting to be the best leader I could, but also not thinking the talents I had were enough. I needed a reality check, and those few moments listening to Viola Davis affirmed my need to appreciate who I was. I refused to continue my journey in leadership disregarding who I'd been created to be. I needed to step into my God-given gifts and trust that I was enough. And if you're anything like the remaining thirty percent of people in that survey I mentioned who don't show up authentically in their roles, chances are you need to do the same. In order to make that shift, you have to magnify the aspects within yourself that set you apart.

One of the best gifts I've ever received was a pearl necklace given to me by my mother when my grandmother passed away. It was one of the few sets that my grandmother kept in her jewelry box. It's a long strand of pink pearls—long enough to wrap around my neck twice. I love the necklace so much that I don't wear it often. Even though you may not see me wear it, it's not unusual for me to simply pick it up and look at it, remembering my grandmother and how she loved to wear it. On the strand, though the pearls appear to be the same shade of pink, they're each different. And while the necklace is uniform for the most part, the pearls that are on the strand each have their own individual characteristics.

I was surprised to find that though there are only five general types of pearls, no one is the same. Each has its own fingerprint. Each has its own shape, bumps, color, and even flaws. Now, when I look at my grandmother's necklace, I don't notice any of the bumps or flaws—only the beauty of the pearls next to each other making a gorgeous piece of jewelry.

Our gifts and talents work the same way. Individually, we each have our own experiences and journeys. We've all made mistakes, and many of them, I'm sure we'd like to forget. We've made some decisions that didn't go as planned, and we've had to overcome challenges and losses. We've also achieved major goals and milestones, and we've celebrated moments with friends and family. Both good and bad, these experiences have shaped us into who we are today. Just like the unique attributes of pearls, you, my friend, are just as beautiful, regal, and unique. And though there may be someone with similar qualities as you, there is no one identical to who you are and what you offer.

Your unique fingerprint makes you who you are. Owning all of the parts of your individual makeup helps you grow in authenticity.

I'm sure you're wondering, *How do I actually do this? Is it possible for me to bravely embrace who I am?* Yes. You have the opportunity to change the path of your journey, and instead of moving farther away from your unique pearl-like qualities, you can run toward each of the characteristics that are woven together to create the masterpiece that you are. There are three practices that I use to ground myself confidently in my gifts. These actions have allowed me to grow, develop, and shine in who I truly am.

○ Get Clear On Your Strengths

"You're so good at framing how things work well together. I didn't even look at things that way until you explained it to me."

I smiled as one of my coaching clients shared this feedback with me. I thanked her and immediately said to myself, *Yes. You're working in your strengths.*

For years, I've always received feedback from supervisors and colleagues about how I am able to help people around me see the bigger picture and vision. I can take smaller pieces of a concept and form one that focuses on an identified goal or destination. This area is a strength for me. Once I was able to identify this as a strength, I felt more at ease when harnessing this area of my leadership in larger settings. Awareness of my strengths gave me the clarity I needed to apply them in various contexts. But, if I didn't know my strengths, I had no understanding of how they could be helpful for myself and others.

Understanding how your strengths work together is key to being empowered to own your talents. How can you be confident in your abilities if you don't know what they are? We often focus on areas where we can improve or attributes we wish we were born with, which usually leads us to feeling inadequate. Instead, if we work from a mindset of abundance, we could more easily tap into all the opportunities we have to bring forth our strengths. Think about it: The last time you were faced with a new challenge in your life, did you immediately tap into your strengths, or did you wish you had another set of skills? A lot of people do the latter. We are laser focused on the talents of other people, and we find it hard to apply this same focus to our own strengths.

You can't implement a skill that you don't know you have. Make a list of your strengths, and consider how often you're amplifying them in your life. Haven't used them lately? Now is the perfect time to flex those muscles and try to work from your strengths.

○ Surround Yourself with Community

I started my podcast, *Rerooted and Thriving,* in August 2021. Though I'd had the idea in 2019, it took me more than two years to actually move forward with launching it. I'd tossed the idea around in my head month after month, and eventually talked myself out of it. I figured the podcast industry was too saturated and mine would get lost in the numerous podcasts available across social media. It wasn't until I had a conversation over brunch with my dear friend Bianca that I decided to move past my own doubts and actually launch it. Her belief in my idea and encouragement to try something new gave me the boost I needed to record the first episode. Now, I'm more than thirty episodes into the podcast, and I couldn't be happier that I did it. There's a strong chance I'd still be thinking about launching if Bianca didn't remind me that I could do it.

I identify as an introvert, and I love spending time on my own, but I also know how important community is in my life. Though I enjoy solo retreats away from crowds, I get energized when I'm around positive people who are encouraging and supportive. Not only has my community encouraged me to take a leap of faith toward my ideas, but they also help me navigate through difficult times. When I face challenges and hard times, I can reach out to them for reminders that things will get better. In those first few years of leadership when I questioned myself the most, it was the affirmations from my supportive network that kept me moving forward.

We all need community. We need people in our corner to support our dreams. We also need people to push back and ask us hard questions. Our community can ground us deeper into owning all that we offer to the world around us.

○ Tap into Your Passions

Oprah once said, "Follow your passion. It will lead you to your purpose."

If you know anything about Oprah, you know that she's lived a life that is full of her passion and purpose. She's been an actress, talk show host, television network owner, school founder, and philanthropist. Her intentionality in every area of her impact demonstrates that she's tapped into her passions. Through my coaching business, I've worked with numerous women who find themselves questioning their purpose. Because they are unsure of their purpose, they question their decisions and exert most of their energy on adopting the goals and aspirations of the people around them. You can't be authentic in who you are if you don't know what your true purpose is. And it's hard to determine your purpose when you don't know where your passions lie. Both your passion and purpose align to give you a foundation to thrive.

I recently served as a guest speaker for a continuing education program in leadership. One of the students in the program asked me, "How do you decide what your next goal is? Do you know what's next for you?"

I paused, smiled, and answered her: "I don't think I have a next big goal in mind, but I do know what I'm passionate about. I'm passionate about empowering people to be unashamed about their expertise. I'm passionate about ensuring there's equitable access to opportunities for people from all walks of life. And as long as my 'next' step aligns with that, then I'm good."

While my leadership journey has allowed me to serve in various capacities, I've always ensured that my passion can be fueled in each of those spaces.

What fuels you? What excites you? I don't take it lightly that we've each been called to live a specific purpose. There's a strong chance that whatever you've been called to do, there's a passion inside of you to bring it to fruition. Don't let that passion go to waste.

What does the authentic *you* look like? Who is that person? Who do you need to be in order to show up fully in your talents every day? Why are you not showing up that way now? What obstacles are keeping you from being proud of your talents? When we work from our natural abilities, we leave the stress that comes with aiming to be someone else, and instead we appreciate the uncommon qualities that make us who we are. We refuse to let ourselves copy everything we see someone else doing. We're able to apply what we learn, but we don't allow what we learn to push us into a space of resentment for the qualities we don't have. How much different would your life look today if you made the decision to be unapologetic about all the gifts you've been blessed with?

I think back on the leader I used to be—questioning my skills and second-guessing my capability. I reflect on how I've grown since then and the growth that has happened to those around me. I know that my leadership has improved immensely because I've gotten clearer on who I am as an authentic leader. And not only am I able to amplify my strengths, but I create space for others consistently to do the same. My goal and my mission as a leader is now encouraging others to tap into the skills that make them unique and to create more impact with who they are in the present moment.

While feeling confident in your own abilities is not an overnight process—it definitely wasn't for me—these steps can assist you in getting there. Over the past six years as an executive, I've grown more comfortable with who I am and more grateful with the natural skills I bring into my role. I think back to that Viola Davis quote, and I smile because I'm arriving at the destination of being brave enough to step outside as who I am. I'm silencing the voices of the naysayers and increasing my inner voice that appreciates who I am. And I'm thankful because I know some people never arrive.

What will it take for you to arrive and
embrace your unique gifts?

Dr. Tamara Wilkerson Dias

As a nonprofit executive director rooted in closing the racial disparity among K–12 teachers, Dr. Tamara Wilkerson Dias has spent nearly a decade in supporting equity in K–12 education. Her passion for supporting and developing others led her to create TWD Coaching and Consulting, which is an equity-focused consulting firm committed to strategic leadership development through actionable and individualized practices in the corporate and nonprofit sectors.

Tamara has been recognized nationally for her work, being named to *Forbes'* 30 Under 30 in Education in 2017 and then named as part of the *Forbes* All Star Alumni list in 2021. She was also named to Charlottesville's 10 under 40 in 2019 for her work in equity throughout the Central Virginia area. She has facilitated workshops and seminars around teacher leadership, sustainability for women in leadership roles, retention practices for nonprofit and corporate organizations, and professional growth practices for educator retention. Tamara believes that once you know your gifts and how to use them, you can walk boldly in your purpose.

Black Pearl

SPRING C JACKSON

"A pearl is a beautiful thing that is produced by an injured life. It is the tear from the injury of the oyster. The treasure of our being in this world is also produced by an injured life. If we had not been wounded, if we had not been injured, then we will not produce the pearl."

—STEPHAN HOELLER

When life has been difficult, it is so very easy to lay down the fight, turn around, quit, or give up on your dreams, landing in a place of complacency or all-out defeat. It takes a lot out of you when you look to outside sources to help, uplift, or save you and no one is coming. Sometimes you must encourage yourself, pick yourself up, dust yourself off, and pick up the pieces, starting over repeatedly if necessary. When life has broken you through trauma, trials, and tribulation, the shifting of your mindset and a pursuit of healing is so essential to get to your life of purpose.

Becoming a childcare provider years ago began my process to get to purpose past the pain and traumas that life had served up. Who knew when I took a job as a childcare professional that it would show me that I had a passion for the safety of children—not only their safety but their development and social emotional well-being because it was not made a priority for me as a child? We all know the extenuating circumstances, pressure, and adversity in society for the African-American family, and mine was no different from any other impoverished family.

Through my own healing journey, I learned that my first experience with trauma was during the age considered early childhood. To shine some light on my own story, my first recollection of trauma was when I experienced an earthquake. I was born in California where these natural disasters occurred often, but this one was clearly a major quake. I was merely three years old, and it is ingrained in my memory forever.

A small brown-face girl whose innocent eyes were wide with terror as she walked out of the kitchen and found her body pinned to the dining room wall. She watched as items were slung across the room back and forth, jumping off glass shelves, and crashing to the floor. Thoughts raced as she wanted to run across the dining room down two short steps into the living room to stop her favorite three-tiered hanging spider plants from swinging back and forth. Why those plants brought so much joy, she still can't remember as an adult, but it may be because she wound up with the green thumb her mother and great-grandmother had. Her plan was diverted as the quake seemed to get worse before it got better, and those plants wound up on the floor with everything else. Something prompted her to get under the dining room table. As her mind returned to being petrified, her body was still pinned to the wall. The thought came again and more urgent this time to get under the table. She finally listened to the prompt and dove under the table until the quake finally stopped after several smaller tremors.

The average quake lasts ten to thirty seconds, but it seemed like forever to an adult, let alone a child of that age. The significance of this story is not even the encounter itself but the lack of experience that should have followed. I can never remember being consoled, soothed, or even as much as hugged to make sure that I was okay. As I search my thoughts for if there were even adults home at the time, my mind holds no recollection of anything that would have seen to it that we were okay in the moments following such a traumatic event. Subsequently, this earliest event and many to follow over the years of my life would be why I have dedicated my influence to the safety, security, and development of children zero to ten years old.

> *Dear is your beauty and priceless you are, as every*
> *black boy and girl who must stand alone*
> *in seas filled with pearls of different sizes and shapes,*
> *but none, none to match their shade.*
> *Black Pearl, you are forced to stand alone, in*
> *classrooms where you have no friend,*
> *on playgrounds where you sit and wish for a friend,*
> *someone clothed in natural ebony, just like you.*
> *Black Pearl, your beauty is radiant, your strength is awesome.*
> *So keep on standing. Stand Tall.*
> *You are Black Pearl.*
> —JENNIFER J. SLATER

In 2005, I took a job at a local childcare facility and worked mostly with the before- and after-school–aged children at different area schools. On occasion, I would fill in with ages zero to five years old for other teachers who were absent. This gave me enough experience and the epiphany that I could provide childcare in my home, which would help because I was without a vehicle of my own at the time. Relying on public transportation with a small child was becoming harder, especially during the winter months, so I set out to find out as much as I possibly could about providing childcare and took my first childcare family while I still lived in a small apartment.

Six years of learning, growing, and educating myself went from providing a place for children to be while their parents worked to a registered childcare home. Obtaining an LLC, Childhood Development Associate (CDA) credential, acquiring industry skills, and permanency turned watching children into a valuable, sought-after childcare business. Moving from that first little apartment into a house that the business seemed to swallow up was the first goal. Then the ambition of being seen as a business owner instead of a babysitter changed drastically in a short period of time. An entire business was birthed out of the need to be able to take care of my children, change my income, and stop relying on public assistance, and at that point, I still was unaware of the true purpose that still welled up inside of me.

After life's ups and down and leaving the industry altogether to take a position as a resource family recruiter, I thought that I had found my calling as a foster care provider. Little did I know that it was only a piece of my story and par for the course. There were those who doubted my ability, said that the market was over saturated, and silently rooted for my downfall, but the only one who truly believed in me was the only one who could put such a desire in my heart and the opportunity right in the palm of my hands. Without Him, there would be no Kingdom Kids Childcare. My doors being opened and even staying open was due to little to no effort of my own. I just did the work, and when doors closed, I believed that at some point my door would open. In the meantime, I was determined to be ready with my oil (Matthew 25:1–13).

It wasn't until at least two years in business that I realized the main mission Kingdom Kids would undertake. It took me even longer to figure out that all this personal passion was birthed through pain. We have a strong commitment to provide premium quality childcare including accessibility and diversity. We exist to attract and maintain client families, and the open-door policy embraces all who desire to provide a better quality of care, preparedness, and education for their children. Kingdom Kids works to provide affordable, first-class care, giving an education by providing a broad range of integrated activities and local community involvement.

Some of the best years of life are spent as a child and later our scholastic years. As adults in a fast-paced society, we sometimes forget just how precious and brief those years are. With that in mind, imagine an alternative to the traditional infant, toddler, preschool, before- and after-school care that not only met your childcare needs, but also provided an activity-based learning environment that encourages learning through play. We are a community of professional caregivers with the credentials to not only enhance your child's early social, emotional, and motor skills, but also to guide them in cognitive and language and emotional development. Also, offered is an inclusive-based curriculum taught in a fun, nurturing caregiving environment. A facility that caters to the low-income families in our community is much needed in our industry. Being the gap-filler childcare for the families and children who are in the most need is not only our priority but seen as our mission. Quality childcare should never be based on income, and we aim to make it possible for every child who enters any of our facilities.

Finding the specific families that I serve came after masterminding with a business coach whose main focus was clarity and alignment. I was in great need of both at the time. It changed my whole business prospective, but the floodgates burst wide open, showing me that the possibilities were endless. If I just buckled down, I could start to get the training needed to flourish in the areas where I needed help the most: the business side of childcare. Preparing a safe, loving environment was a strength that needed no polishing, but longevity in the center childcare arena was a must to reach all the overwhelming goals God had place on my heart. *Whew…* It is quite the feat, but I am up for the challenge as long as it is a God idea instead of just a good idea. I know that He will hold my hand the whole way and see me through all of it.

The world is your oyster. It is up to you to find the pearls.
—CHRIS GARDNER

As a childcare owner, I have been through hell and high water by way of management issues, no systems, financial instability, and extremely high employee turnover among so many other things. The story of how I acquired my first location is nothing short of a testimony. A long story, a little less long: I was let go from my job as a front desk manager, a position that I held and worked very hard at for a little over two years. The next year receiving unemployment, I made a job out of going to the library daily and preparing to open a childcare someday. Under the impression that there was no way that all of that work hadn't prepared me, I sought the building that I am in now. Passed over for another person and disappointed, I wrote it off as there must be something better for me. Was there ever, and almost another full year went by until I got a call from that same landlord.

Now keep in mind the ten months had been stressful from barely being able to pay rent and spending most of the previous winter without a vehicle after wearing my truck out driving Uber. Spending an entire summer without lights and consequently air conditioning and eventually getting that vehicle repossessed was a bit rough, but there was always a ram in the bush. I was able to get my old job back working overnight, allowing me to get some relief from the heat and eat most days. When they came to get my car, I emptied it, called a friend to ask for a ride to work later, and went back to bed. Putting my worries in God's hands had never been so easy. I was truly over the fight—trying to find every way that I could think of to fix things. After surrendering things to Him for the second time in my life, rest was attainable.

By that next fall, I received the call that changed my life. Asleep when the call came, I woke up and checked my messages and could not believe it. The voice recording said something like, "I was wondering if you were still interested in being a childcare owner. If you haven't found another building, the current lease holder is no longer interested in being a childcare owner and wants out of the business."

I almost choked listening to the message. I thought, *Of course I want this building!*

I had my eye on this business years before I ever truly knew that I would be a childcare center owner, not knowing why it always stuck out to me. In that moment, I told God that if this was His idea, He was going to have to do it. I had enough money for my November rent coming up and that was all. I remember laying back down after calling to leave the landlord a message with a smile on my face thinking, *God's got it.*

Well, He most definitely showed up and showed out. The lady relinquishing her business did almost every bit of the legwork to get me in there and her out. She went above and beyond with all the paperwork, pulled out all of the stops pooling her resources to make the entire thing happen. As for the money needed to get started, she took all of the income that was collected from current families and paid her initial payment, the rent, and insurance and left me with all of the bills paid so that there was no debt going in. I took control of the business two days after my birthday after her cutting me a check with a full ride of staff and almost a building full of children. Needless to say, it was the best birthday gift that I have received to date. My acquiring my first location has not come without a lot of stress, growing pains, and lessons learned, but it has unquestionably prepared me for the next phase in my career, which is currently under way.

Through my research, it is my finding that a lack of access to high-quality, affordable childcare continues to drive parents out of the workforce, disproportionately affecting women's and low-income families' careers. The trend especially affects minority women. It has been reported that they would look for the higher paying jobs if they had better access to childcare. I found that this was true for me as a single parent with young children. Looking back over my own happenstances, it rendered me being forced to take jobs that did not accentuate my skills or that did not have any room for advancement. Also, the lack of transportation and reliable childcare kept me locked into that dead-end employment until my children were old enough to go to elementary school, where they were close enough to be walked, or we could rely on the school transportation system. Those days are over, and taking my experience and coupling them with studies is shaping a program that will benefit owners, operators, and most importantly the children and families that we serve.

Childcare directors know from experience that decisions made in one area of the company will affect the rest of the organization. Directors who understand the business side can operate more effectively and respond faster to the market trends, as the organizations of the twenty-first century will demand that the internal departments be interconnected. In the same way, childcare owners who understand the skills, knowledge, and techniques needed to support children's development and learning can design and support high-quality programs with their administrative decisions. As different states develop guidelines to cover skills and knowledge children are expected to learn, both sides of the business of childcare must work together to meet the expectations of what children should learn before entering elementary school.

Childcare can and has been a tough business to run if you don't run it like a business. Through my encounters over the last three years, as well as my more than sixteen years in childcare, it has more than qualified me to help other childcare owners grow and scale their businesses. If you allow your clients and teachers to run you ragged and you don't market hard enough or at all, then you run the risk of closing your doors and leaving the industry defeated. This will never happen to any of our locations or clients as long as there is still breath in my body. A strategically compiled team and Super Friends with my leadership are on a mission to impact as many children as possible through owners who have quality leadership, full enrollment, marketing and who execute better business practices. We don't believe in making things appear to be something they are not; however, we remain confident. Although this industry is absolutely a tough business, we not only believe but know that childcare can be equally as profitable and rewarding with strategic planning, systems, and all components working together like a well-oiled machine, proving that one does not have to be an omission of the other. With a solid organization, programs can adapt to changing conditions and withstand uncertainty.

While childcare has been my passion for many years, its influence on my life has given me that ability to mold, shape, support, and influence the lives of many others over the years. Being a community resource and allowing me to employ people is humbling. A heartfelt thank you goes out to the many people who have helped to shape me, pour into me, and who have supported me getting to this amazing place in my life. There is only up from here, and my prayer is that I can help to influence others in the ways that the intelligent, encouraging, and influential people have done for me throughout the first leg of my journey. Life has not been easy, but no one said that it would be. If I hadn't been met with so much adversity, I may have never stumbled upon my strength, true passion, and purpose in life.

Spring C Jackson

Spring C Jackson is the Winners Circle Childcare Consultant, published author, and speaker. With more than eighteen years of experience in the childcare field, she began her journey as a center childcare provider, in-home small business owner, and resource family recruiter, and is now the owner and chief executive officer of Kingdom Kids Childcare, LLC.

She has extensive training and has held a CDA in childcare. Spring is currently exploring expansion plans to create a network of Kingdom Kids branches across the United States through ownership and franchising. The mission is to provide the same quality care as higher end centers to lower income families, filling the gap for those children who need it most.

In addition, she has moved into coaching and consulting to help current childcare owners to scale their childcare businesses. A trailblazer in her own right, Spring is a believer in going where there is no path and leaving a trail. She lives by the mantra, "If only to be different"—a guiding principle that embraces originality and authenticity in all things. Allow her to remind you of these pearls of wisdom from an unknown author: "It's not so much what you say that counts, it's how you make people feel."

Feel free to contact her at info@springcjackson.com. Please take a look at her website springcjackson.com and or kingdomkidscare.com. Thank you.

Riding the
Waves of Wellness

PENNY MCPHERSON

The Caribbean ocean water was bathtub warm with a turquoise tint. I soaked up the sun as my feet sank into the soft sand. I almost died that day. I was in the mighty ocean waters up to my shoulders, and I could not swim.

Growing up in Richmond, Virginia, I never learned to swim, therefore, I have a healthy fear of the ocean. So, when my husband, Paul, and I moved to a funky little beach town on the Caribbean coast of Costa Rica, I resisted going deep into the water for many months. During certain times of the year, surfers came from all over the world to surf the waves on nearby beaches while others gathered shells in hopes of finding pearls. The rainforest met the beach where we lived among the sloths, monkeys, and giant iguanas. There was no hospital in our tiny town, and we shopped for groceries on our bicycle.

On the days I embraced ocean therapy, I sat in shallow water practicing my deep breathing while schools of fish darted around me. After some months, the warm, rhythmic turquoise waters beckoned me, and I became comfortable with the ocean. Paul is a strong man and swimmer, so I was content with holding his hand when venturing into deeper water. I used my tried-and-true stress management techniques to avoid panicking at approaching waves and to calm my heart rate when I felt the power of the ocean. We loved the way the motions of the waves enveloped our bodies.

I encourage you to safely experience the ocean because the sound of the waves is therapeutic. It relaxes our brains and stimulates the body's production of happy hormones such as serotonin and dopamine.

Each time we stepped out of the rainforest onto the beach, we were usually the only ones there. During these times, we loved feeling like the entire ocean was all ours, waving at the occasional passersby walking their fur babies.

One day I was holding Paul's hand, riding the waves, and the water was up to my shoulders—still a little nervous, but I was having fun and comfortable. We were singing water-themed gospel songs. Singing helped keep my mind off the fact that I could not swim and the ocean had the power to swallow me. If a wave approached that was too high for me to jump, Paul would lift me like a ballet dancer.

"Weee," I exclaimed.

The waves kept coming, and then they calmed. I turned my back, admiring the beauty of the giant coconut tree branches waving in unison in the bright blue sky. And then it happened: I heard the words that struck fear into my soul.

My capable, strong swimmer of a husband said, "Uh-oh."

I knew by his tone, that he was not going to be able to help me with this wave. Still holding his hand, I looked just in time to see an eight-foot wave cresting right at us. The last thing I heard him yell was, "Hold on."

However, the powerful wave ripped our grip apart, and I was engulfed in what felt like a giant front load washer, tumbling over and over in a powerful wave. I had no control over what was happening to me. If I gasped or panicked, I might die. I was no longer riding the waves going with the flow.

I was no longer in my comfort zone. I was alone, fighting for my life under the water. I was fighting against the wave trying to get where I thought was up so that Paul could see me and save me. I was fighting against the wave trying to get my bearings so maybe I could stand.

It reminds me of my wellness journey where sometimes I had to fight to not just survive, but to thrive.

Let's flash back to find out why I even needed to journey to wellness success.

I was plant-based in the eighties when the Impossible Burger was impossible to find. I have been on and off this journey for decades, but I finally uncovered pearls of wisdom that helped me live a sustainable healthier lifestyle. I transformed from sick and stressed to wellness success using these wellness pearls and the acronym SOW.

The S in SOW represents societal norms. Whenever you make a change in your life, other people will mind your business. They will question why you are making changes in areas that don't pertain to their success. Why are you eating, wearing, doing that? Why are you going against the grain?

I choose to let God order my steps and author my story. There is a quote that says, "When you write the story of your life, don't let anyone else hold the pen." No one can walk in your truth except you. Society said that I should go to college, get a job, earn six figures, wear high heels, and retire. Instead, I took a personal timeout, chose a global education, increased my longevity, and wore sandals for 365 days a year. My only regret is not doing it sooner.

I wrote a magazine article called "No Regret Life," and in it, I talk about wanting to live on purpose. In my area of focus, this means striving for abundant health now to have less regrets later in life. When you decide to improve your lifestyle, be confident in the decision. Be committed to yourself enough to think outside of the popular opinion, recycled perspective, and swim against the current.

Societal norms will tell us that it is normal to have heart disease, elevated cholesterol, constipation, and not sleep well. It will tell you soaking hot flashes or debilitating allergies are acceptable, and for every aliment, the remedy is to take a pill and pay a bill. Since representation matters, it's important to note, according to a Pew Research Center survey, eight percent of African Americans identify as vegan or vegetarian compared to three percent of the general population. I am so proud of my brothers and sisters joining this health journey. I welcome anyone on this path to better health. We must all keep in mind there are systems in place that are adroitly designed to influence the way we think, buy, and consume. It is also fascinating when you change your lifestyle, everyone suddenly becomes experts in why your choice for your body will not work. Family, friends, and strangers will offer their unsolicited opinions. Whether you decide to drink or eat healthier, do not let anyone dissuade you.

The first pearl of wisdom is to make courageous choices for your health.

The O stands for original foods. I have a signature presentation called Plant-Based for Newbies because one of the first strategies to look, live, and feel well is to investigate the ingredient label and not the marketing labels of foods. The marketing labels are not always true. Labels have pretty pictures of fruits and vegetables, but you may be consuming carcinogenic foods. Even more likely, you may be consuming "food like" products that don't support the functions that keep you vibrant and healthy.

One client told me she was tired of not having enough energy. When she started consuming original foods—foods that grow from the ground— she really noticed an improvement in her energy levels. Whole foods—real foods that are plant-based—give us energy and mental clarity. Improving your diet will help you think more clearly. The majority of our diet should consist of vegetables, fruits, grains, legumes, beans, nuts, and seeds. There are thousands of diverse types of foods that restore and rejuvenate our bodies. Don't believe the hype that you must have animal food to thrive. The first step to an abundantly healthy lifestyle is increasing original foods in your daily food repertoire.

Research shows vegetables and whole grains assimilate at a slower pace. Because fruits are fiber-rich, a person feels fuller longer and cravings decrease. Currently, cravings are rewiring our brains to think we need more food when we do not. The more plant focused our diets are, the less we crave highly processed foods. Remarkably, after a raw detox, my bloating and salty and sweet cravings unmistakably subside. Eating when we are craving and not hungry can lead to obesity, which is a contributing factor for chronic diseases. People whose diet consists primarily of plant food sources have a much lower chance of being obese. Their risk of having severe heart diseases, living with Type 2 diabetes, stroke, cancer, or other fatal diseases diminishes greatly.

It's important to understand what we consume is not just what we eat. It also includes the internal conversations we have with ourselves. We can be our own worst critic. Original foods can be edible. What we feed our minds elevates or deflates our chances for success. If our mindset says, *I can never live a healthier lifestyle,* this will be our truth. Conversely, if we believe making small changes of increasing fruits and vegetables is possible, we are more apt to sustain the change. What we consume will help us move toward ease or toward dis-ease. Dis-ease is a concept where the body lacks something to rest at a state of optimal health. Disease is a diagnosis. Choices we feed our body and our minds move us toward ease.

At one point in life, I was paying my hard-earned money for sick management, spending valuable time at medical offices, popping too many pills, and I needed to make changes. I was being tossed about with health issues. I ignored the waves of extra weight. I had to get off the couch. I ignored the waves of change in unchecked stress.

We are managing bills, family issues, microaggressions, insecurities, and other people's problems. We need to monitor the avenues to our overall well-being. The second pearl of wisdom is consume what best feeds your soul.

I transformed by using the W in S.O.W.: Make your *wellness* a priority. I started sharing my health journey years ago after I made it a priority. As I approach my well-seasoned years free of prescription medications, I am committed to prioritizing wellness. I have lost count of the number of wellness fads I have tried—and failed. I needed to leave the never-ending cycle of being sick, hospital bills, pills, rinse, and repeat. Prioritize your wellness over everything else—yes, including your job, friends, and family. Find ways to schedule yourself into your everyday life. Most people never regret making wellness a priority. If you don't take care of you, you will be overcome with the waves of illness and disease and unable to take care of anyone else.

That day in the ocean having fun overshadowed the consideration of safety. I should have departed the ocean when Paul had to continually lift me because the waves were getting higher and higher. I ignored the warnings because I was comfortable.

I should have made healthy choices in my lifestyle when I was young, but I didn't know better. I should have made better choices in college, but I put it off. I should have noticed I was slipping deeper into the depths when the number of medications, sick visits, and tests increased, but I was not paying attention. Dr. Maya Angelou said, "The need for change, bull-dozed a road down the center of my mind." When we realize the necessity of change, we will do all within our power to reach our goal.

I started on my wellness journey because I had a need for change. I wanted to stop supporting the systems that profited from my overweight, sick, and stressed being. I wanted to be healthier as much as I wanted to breathe when I was underwater. For the first time, I was priority number one. I declared I would reclaim my health despite the raised eyebrows of people in their own comfort zones.

I must admit, over the years, I fell back into bad habits due to the influence of others, but not anymore. I remember long ago I told one doctor I would try this plant-based thing. She said she could not advise that. I would become diabetic because I was pre-diabetic. I would have to have organs removed, more tests, and medication for the rest of my life. She stated that as we get older, these things happen. I left, sat in my car, and cried. I was tired of sinking into sickness with no sustainable results.

The third pearl of wisdom is sickness becomes a priority when we don't prioritize health.

I must recognize the good doctors who acknowledged my efforts and said we could wait to see what my lifestyle results were. I would advise communicating with your health professional and find one who can partner with you on the journey. I was tired of the mounting list of issues such as allergies, pains, hormones, auto-immune, and digestive issues. I tried the traditional methods, and they led to medicines that managed the symptoms. The great news is it catapulted my wellness journey. I treated my wellness education as seriously as my college education. I systematically educated myself to maintain my path to wellness. I transitioned from pescatarian to vegetarian to ultimately plant-based. I am a living testimony of how I reaped incredible mental and physical results. Full stop.

There are many vegan or plant-based eaters who are unkind to those who are in a different place on their journey. Your diet does not make you a saint. We should be passionate yet compassionate in this ministry. I am not perfect-based Penny, I am Plant Based Penny, not where I ought to be, but not where I used to be.

Remember this important point: To receive the full benefit of a healthy lifestyle transformation, understand it encompasses more than consuming food. It also incorporates the natural components of air, sunlight, sleep, water, love, and stress management. This comprehensive holistic approach is how you can secure the greatest gain of living a healthier lifestyle. Wisdom pearl number four is a healthy lifestyle transcends food.

In my health journey, it took a little over a year, but the doctors decreased and discontinued medications. After making wellness my priority, the abundance of clarity experienced lead to unimaginable freedom. No longer under a doctor's care for chronic disease or illness, I uncovered new opportunities. I had the privilege to not just think outside the box, but to think unconventionally and ask for life-changing questions.

What would I regret later if I didn't do it? Where is God blessing, and let's go there? The answer led me to dislodge from life in the United States.

No worries about filling prescriptions or routine medical appointments in a foreign land. What was impossible became possible, and I have made fantastic indelible memories.

In the past twenty years, I remember being too busy to deal with diagnoses, which came in waves from test results. I ignored the creeping weight gain and minor health setbacks. I ignored the waves. Eight years ago, more waves of unwelcome news came with a proclamation that it would just get worse. The doctor had said my pre-diabetes would eventually turn into full-blown diabetes as I aged. Not only am I no longer pre-diabetic, but my previous bad cholesterol levels are also normal. But wait, there's more: My protein, iron, calcium, kidney functions, and vitamin D levels are normal. Although living abroad in different countries and continents was fantastic, living abroad did not make me healthy. The secret was in every plant-yielding seed and every fruit with seeds given by God as referenced in Genesis 1:29. A proper plant-based lifestyle is holistically nourishing.

I was tossed by the waves of sickness and stress. I wasted years focused on what I might give up instead of what I might gain. Put this on your refrigerator: Nothing tastes as good as good health feels.

Remember the story: I was overcome by the waves. I had life-or-death choices to make. I could focus on where was my husband, Paul, and why didn't he save me. I could focus on the fact that I kept getting tossed about by waves. I could focus on why me, why now. I could control none of those things.

Remember the serenity prayer? "God grant me the serenity to accept the things I cannot change, change the things I can, and the wisdom to know the difference." That day was indicative of my wellness journey. I chose to focus on what I could control. I knew that even though Paul's arms could not reach me, God's arms were not too short, and He did not bring me this far to leave me. I utilized a breath-work technique I learned while in school in Costa Rica. I knew I was able to hold my breath for at least one minute. I practiced this technique often, so when the initial wave hit, I instinctively held my breath, and my brain automatically started counting. I knew if I did not reach my breath limit underwater, I could remain calm. In my peaceful turbulence, I found clarity. I needed to stop fighting against the power of the waves. I was no match. Instead, I embraced the power and used what was at my disposal. The next time that powerful wave came upon me, I positioned myself to use the energy to propel myself forward. This allowed this non swimmer to get to my knees, then to my feet. As I was standing, still with my eyes closed, gasping welcomed breaths, Paul was there shielding me and blocking the relentless onslaught of ocean waves with his body while I collected myself. I changed my focus and lived.

Before leaving the states, in a follow-up doctor's appointment when my test results were drastically improved, my doctor said, "I don't know what you're doing, but keep doing it."

I hope you will join me focusing on what is within our control. Learn to S.O.W. When it comes to your wellness, live beyond *societal norms* and make courageous choices for your health. Focus on *original* foods and consume what best feeds your body and soul. Designate *wellness* as your priority because sickness becomes a priority when we don't prioritize health.

I am humbled to be able to share these pearls along the path to wellness. It is so gratifying to hear from my family of happy clients who move from problems to progress. Recently this queen mother shared, "I am so grateful. The natural way is the way to go. No pain. I been torturing myself trying this and that, and I just praise the Lord that I found you. You don't know how much the Lord answered that prayer. It's more than a blessing. Thank you, Lord, that you showed me. Thank you, and I praise you."

Testimonies like this one remind me of the lyrics in the song written by Alma Bazel Androzzo that say, "If I can help somebody, as I travel along… my living shall not be in vain."

Like the ocean waves, the waves of life are going to come. We must position ourselves to be our best health advocates and pass along the knowledge. We are fearfully and wonderfully made to look, live, and feel well. There is an old African proverb that says, "Knowledge is better than wealth. You have to look after wealth, but knowledge looks after you."

Be well, family.

Penny McPherson

Penny McPherson, also known as Plant Based Penny, recently returned to the United States after living abroad in Central and South America on a two-year time-out. Penny embraces the holistic approach to healing and living a healthier lifestyle. She studied and successfully practiced natural healing with plants, natural elements, and medicinal techniques on three continents and seven countries.

Penny enjoyed a successful career as a senior leader and vice president for a global bank. She earned her bachelor's degree in business administration from High Point University, the Competent Communicator Certification from Toastmasters International, and graduated from Leadership Metro Richmond. She studied abroad at the Refugio Medical Missionary School and Hidden Gardens Wellness Center in Costa Rica. She also studied cooking skills at Southern Kitchen's Cooking School. In addition, she practices holistic methods and strategies learned from leading global authorities in Singapore, the Philippines, Panama, Costa Rica, Colombia, and more.

Penny uses her platforms to empower others in the use of plants as medicine, following a comprehensive healthy lifestyle and "fooducation." She also pays homage to natural wellness methods our grandmothers utilized.

Penny has been seen in Mitchell Productions, the I Am This Woman broadcast, Comcast TV, Freedom Locs Podcast, Christian Traveler's Podcast, Black Expats Living Abroad, Alpha Kappa Alpha Sorority, Inc., Vitamix, Lemonade Mindset, Ephesus SDA Church, When We Pray Ministries, Good Foods Grocery, the Fifty-Plus Association, and more.

Rural Virginia is now home with Paul, her king and husband. Her lifestyle includes reducing her environmental impact through the sustainable living practices of gardening, recycling, and sewing. Penny's goals are a year-round garden, a homestead retreat, and animals. She says, "It is my passion to use my God-given skills and wisdom to help you look, live, and feel well."

Her favorite Bible text is James 1:5: "If you need wisdom, ask our generous God, and He will give it to you. He will not rebuke you for asking."

Her personal quote is, "God made me, and He does not make mistakes. Therefore, I can do, I can learn, I can succeed."

Penny is available for one-on-one consultations and speaking engagements.

Email: Life@plantbasedpennylife.com
Website: PlantBasedPennyLife.com
Facebook page and group: facebook.com/plantbasedpennylife
Instagram: instagram.com/PlantBasedPennyLife
Business phone: 434-265-6061

You can be Dynamic Despite Dysfunction

KATHERINE L. STATEN

*T*his chapter is one taken from my recent book, Descendants of Dysfunction.

In my book, *Descendants of Dysfunction: What we can learn from the Bible's dysfunctional families*, I use abbreviated stories of dysfunctional biblical families to build bridges of connection to modern-day family dysfunction.

My study of adverse childhood experiences and the lasting negative effect of early trauma brought science to what I already knew, that stress and trauma can kill—physically, emotionally, and in many other ways. This is what compelled me to write my first book, and the stories of biblical families provide excellent content on family dysfunction.

While this story may be familiar to you, I want to bring the emotions of the family members into focus. How do negative emotions linger and impact relationships as we move forward? These are not transactional events. Yes, these things happened, and the plan of God was always fulfilled, but for example, how did Joseph feel as he processed the hate and disregard his brothers had for him? How did he handle success, from a place of bitterness or from a place of integrity, respect, and love? I would liken Joseph's love and care for the brothers who turned on him to the world's most famous pearl that is known as La Peregrina, which means The Incomparable. His love and care for his family after such a betrayal is extraordinary. Also, pay attention to how you feel, what you learn, and how that knowledge can be impactful in your life and the lives of others.

We know biblical times are not like the times we live in today, but how can we use the experience of this biblical family to help us today to recognize family dysfunction and develop healthy patterns that we can model for generations to come? Having more than thirty years of professional experience serving people in human service programs, I have a keen awareness of the real issues that individuals and families face. I have always advocated for the needs of people—for them to reach their highest potential.

Many times, what is holding us back cannot be seen or quantified. It is the effects of unaddressed individual, family, community, and historical trauma. Seeing these needs, I launched Flourish and Grow to promote trauma consciousness and healing from early adversity. My dream is for everyone to be able to approach trauma and grief and triumph.

This chapter is not intended to be psychological advice. It is not a substitute for professional clinical expertise or treatment.

For questions about specific family issues, please seek advice from a qualified provider of family and/or mental health services.

This chapter takes us on a lifelong journey to fulfill a dream and a great family reunion. It is important because it models how to respond in love after being mistreated by your own family. It is important because it tells the story of being despised by those who are supposed to love you, enduring hardship, and eventually being elevated by strangers who recognize the greatness God has placed inside of you.

The referenced scripture is from the New Living Translation of the Holy Bible.

○ Referenced Scripture

Genesis 37:1–36

1 So Jacob settled again in the land of Canaan, where his father had lived as a foreigner.

2 This is the account of Jacob and his family. When Joseph was seventeen years old, he often tended his father's flocks. He worked for his half brothers, the sons of his father's wives Bilhah and Zilpah. But Joseph reported to his father some of the bad things his brothers were doing.

3 Jacob loved Joseph more than any of his other children because Joseph had been born to him in his old age. So one day Jacob had a special gift made for Joseph—a beautiful robe. 4 But his brothers hated Joseph because their father loved him more than the rest of them. They couldn't say a kind word to him.

5 One night Joseph had a dream, and when he told his brothers about it, they hated him more than ever. 6 "Listen to this dream," he said. 7 "We were out in the field, tying up bundles of grain. Suddenly my bundle stood up, and your bundles all gathered around and bowed low before mine!"

8 His brothers responded, "So you think you will be our king, do you? Do you actually think you will reign over us?" And they hated him all the more because of his dreams and the way he talked about them.

9 Soon Joseph had another dream, and again he told his brothers about it. "Listen, I have had another dream," he said. "The sun, moon, and eleven stars bowed low before me!"

10 This time he told the dream to his father as well as to his brothers, but his father scolded him. "What kind of dream is that?" he asked. "Will your mother and I and your brothers actually come and bow to the ground before you?" 11 But while his brothers were jealous of Joseph, his father wondered what the dreams meant.

12 Soon after this, Joseph's brothers went to pasture their father's flocks at Shechem. 13 When they had been gone for some time, Jacob said

to Joseph, "Your brothers are pasturing the sheep at Shechem. Get ready, and I will send you to them."

"I'm ready to go," Joseph replied.

14 "Go and see how your brothers and the flocks are getting along," Jacob said. "Then come back and bring me a report." So Jacob sent him on his way, and Joseph traveled to Shechem from their home in the valley of Hebron.

15 When he arrived there, a man from the area noticed him wandering around the countryside. "What are you looking for?" he asked.

16 "I'm looking for my brothers," Joseph replied. "Do you know where they are pasturing their sheep?"

17 "Yes," the man told him. "They have moved on from here, but I heard them say, 'Let's go on to Dothan.'" So Joseph followed his brothers to Dothan and found them there.

○ Joseph Sold into Slavery

18 When Joseph's brothers saw him coming, they recognized him in the distance. As he approached, they made plans to kill him. 19 "Here comes the dreamer!" they said. 20 "Come on, let's kill him and throw him into one of these cisterns. We can tell our father, 'A wild animal has eaten him.' Then we'll see what becomes of his dreams!"

21 But when Reuben heard of their scheme, he came to Joseph's rescue. "Let's not kill him," he said. 22 "Why should we shed any blood? Let's just throw him into this empty cistern here in the wilderness. Then he'll die without our laying a hand on him." Reuben was secretly planning to rescue Joseph and return him to his father.

23 So when Joseph arrived, his brothers ripped off the beautiful robe he was wearing. 24 Then they grabbed him and threw him into the cistern. Now the cistern was empty; there was no water in it. 25 Then, just as they were sitting down to eat, they looked up and saw a caravan of camels in the distance coming toward them. It was a group of Ishmaelite traders taking a load of gum, balm, and aromatic resin from Gilead down to Egypt.

26 Judah said to his brothers, "What will we gain by killing our brother? We'd have to cover up the crime. 27 Instead of hurting him, let's sell him to those Ishmaelite traders. After all, he is our brother—our own flesh and blood!" And his brothers agreed. 28 So when the Ishmaelites, who were Midianite traders, came by, Joseph's brothers pulled him out of the cistern and sold him to them for twenty pieces of silver. And the traders took him to Egypt.

29 Some time later, Reuben returned to get Joseph out of the cistern. When he discovered that Joseph was missing, he tore his clothes in grief. 30 Then he went back to his brothers and lamented, "The boy is gone! What will I do now?"

31 Then the brothers killed a young goat and dipped Joseph's robe in its blood. 32 They sent the beautiful robe to their father with this message: "Look at what we found. Doesn't this robe belong to your son?"

33 Their father recognized it immediately. "Yes," he said, "it is my son's robe. A wild animal must have eaten him. Joseph has clearly been torn to pieces!" 34 Then Jacob tore his clothes and dressed himself in burlap. He mourned deeply for his son for a long time. 35 His family all tried to comfort him, but he refused to be comforted. "I will go to my grave mourning for my son," he would say, and then he would weep.

36 Meanwhile, the Midianite traders arrived in Egypt, where they sold Joseph to Potiphar, an officer of Pharaoh, the king of Egypt. Potiphar was captain of the palace guard.

○ Story of This Family

Jacob continued the same favoritism in his own home as his parents, Isaac and Rebecca. Jacob favored Joseph, one of his sons. Joseph was the first of two sons born to Rachel, Jacob's favorite wife. To show the favor on Joseph, his father, Jacob, made him a fancy coat of many colors. His brothers were jealous of the favoritism of this son, and when they got a chance to get rid of Joseph, they did.

In addition to Jacob's favor, Joseph, a dreamer, interprets his own dreams and told his brothers and father that they would bow down to him one day. Can you imagine that you, the favorite son… Isn't it enough to be the favorite son, and you will rule over us, too? It was too much for the brothers to consider. When they had the opportunity, they got rid of Joseph by selling him into slavery and bringing that coat of many colors back to their father with the blood of goats on it.

Jacob, believing that Joseph had been killed, grieved for his favorite son. Joseph experienced much hardship. He was sold into slavery by his brothers. He was put in jail, only to rise to the highest level in the kingdom. This lets us know that favor and giftedness do not exempt us from hardship. As history would unfold, many years later, Joseph's dream would come to fruition. He would reign over his brothers, and they would indeed bow down to him.

○ What Made Them Dysfunctional?

Siblings compete out of necessity. They compete for the love and attention of their parents. Imagine, you are not the favorite child, and nothing you do or say can change that. Out of desperation, you might do something drastic, like act out or lash out against the favorite child. The dysfunction in this family was at an all-time high due to the favoritism and preference that Joseph had with his father, Jacob. For the other sons, it was no use trying. No matter what they did, they would never measure up to Joseph. In their desperation, this would make concocting evil schemes and, for all purposes, lying about what happened to Joseph a plan that the brothers agreed to.

○ What Made This Family Strong?

Despite favoritism, pride, and jealousy, God allowed Joseph, a former slave and prisoner, to be in a position to preserve this family for God's purpose.

God was able to help Joseph overcome his own painful past and provide a way for the family who betrayed him. It took many years, but now everyone can see that Joseph's dream came true.

○ Is This Your Family?

If this is your family, take steps to be dynamic. Whenever you can, reduce the stress in your life. Chronic stress affects every system in our bodies. The result of prolonged stress helps to make us weak and less able to fight off illnesses and diseases. Use stress management tools such as deep breathing and mindfulness. Make a list of relaxing things that you like to do, and make it a point to do these things as often as possible. Develop healthy skills that help you to be more self-aware. Get in tune with your gifts and talents, and take steps to develop in those areas. Live life in the present. Reject the need to go back and change things. No matter how much you replay the past, you won't be able to change it. But if you want, you can change today and future days. Spend your days building a healthy future with your loved ones and friends. Dwelling on your anger, pain, and past resentment won't propel you toward the greatness in your life. Live in the present, and make most of your future.

Joseph was dynamic, despite his family dysfunction and the difficulty he faced throughout his life.

He knew he was special, even if it was only in the eyes of his father, but instantly he was thrown into the position of a slave when his brothers sold him to the Ishmaelites. He was loved and rejected in the same house.

In Egypt, he was sold to Potiphar. He was a slave, but Joseph had so many things going for him. The Lord was with him, and everything he did went well. He had favor with God and man. His master Potiphar trusted him as a hard working and faithful servant. Having been blessed in his father's house and now living as a slave, Joseph could have had a bad attitude and expected much to come to him, but he worked hard and could be trusted.

God even saw to it that Potiphar was blessed because Joseph was there. Joseph didn't let his youth and comely looks get the best of him. He had a healthy fear of God that allowed him to not sin against God with Potiphar's wife. Even after all of this, Joseph was lied on and put in prison. God was still with him. As a prisoner, he was put in charge of the other prisoners. He helped others to be restored, but once restored, they forgot about him. When he got his chance, he took full advantage of his God-given gifts, talents, and abilities and gave God all the credit due to Him.

There was no shrinking back to make others feel comfortable. He interpreted Pharaoh's dream and had the solution to save Egypt, other nations, and even his own family from the impending famine. Joseph was put in charge again. He could have been bitter after being unjustly imprisoned, but a bitter, discontented attitude does not a good leader make. Widen your lens and look at the big picture. The purposes of God are always bigger than us—bigger than we can imagine. Through his wisdom and administrative gift, he implemented the planning and preparation to save nations.

God has a plan for pain and suffering. God can use difficulty for good. Joseph was seventeen years old when he was sold as a slave and thirty when he rode in the second chariot of Pharaoh as ruler over all of Egypt. Joseph married an Egyptian woman, Asenath, who bore two sons, Manasseh and Ephraim. As Joseph had interpreted, the seven years of plenty were followed by seven years of famine.

A lifetime had passed before there would be a peculiar family reunion. People from every nation would get the word that there was food in Egypt. Joseph's brothers would be among those who would seek food there, but they had no idea that the brother they sold into slavery many years ago would be the one who would literally spare their lives from the famine.

At that moment, Joseph was not worried about the past, the hardship he endured, whose fault it was, and how he could get sweet revenge. God gave him more blessings that far outweighed his trouble. He was looking ahead to the future. He was looking ahead to the life he could have with his family there by his side and the life he could now share with them because the favor of God was on his life.

God gave him a chance to see his family again and put him in the position to care for them during the famine. When you know the blessing of God is on your life, there is no reason for revenge or retaliation. As their father, Jacob, spelled out before his death in Genesis chapter 49, each son would get what he had coming to him, and God would make sure of that.

Yes, Joseph was truly dynamic, although he experienced family dysfunction in his formative years. To be dynamic is to be powerful, effective, energetic, and strong.

As you consider ways to heal, thrive, and live a dynamic life consider the following:

○ D—Define Yourself by Grace

Our definition of ourselves affects everything we do and think. When we define ourselves by grace, we learn that we measure up. We learn to stop beating ourselves up. We learn that instead of God's judgment and condemnation, we can accept God's blessings and favor. We are not defined by what someone else has done to us or by the mistakes we have made. When I define myself by grace, I am a new creature. Read 2 Corinthians 5:17, Colossians 2:10–14, and Romans 8:31–39.

○ Y- Yield to Your Response, Not Your Reaction

You may ask what's the difference between a response and a reaction. Reactions are usually made with the emotions leading the way. We may react out of anger or fear. I encourage you to respond instead of reacting. Pause and consider these questions: Is my reaction right for the time and place? Is it right for the situation? Would I want the same type of treatment that I am ready to dish out? Is my reaction moral with integrity? What are the long-term effects of my reaction?

Instead of reacting, yield or give over to a slowed-down response. You may want to react but yield to your thought process. If you have to, count to ten. Every time you learn to moderate your responses, you begin to set and establish new patterns of thinking and calming yourself down.

○ N– Nurture Your Transformed Mind

Don't conform to old ways of thinking that don't serve you well. As believers, we are commanded to transform and renew our minds. Read Romans 12:2. Our patterns of thinking should align with God's way and perfect will for our lives. Read Philippians 4:8. In the Bible, a good mind is described as a ready, humble, and fervent mind. Read Acts 17:11, 20:19, and 2 Corinthians 7:7. God wants to engage our intellect and transform our minds to gain knowledge and understanding so we can apply wisdom to the blueprint of our lives.

○ A–Use Affirmations

I purpose to break the cycle of sin by developing discernment, self-control, and yielding myself to God (2 Peter 1:2–11). I believe there is no temptation too great for me to bear with God's help (1 Corinthians 10:13). I choose blessings over bitterness (Hebrews 12:15). I will cooperate with God by yielding to him (Romans 12:1–2). I will allow God to heal my wounded spirit. I am grateful for the love of God that equates my value with a jewel, a sheep, a silver coin, and a sun.

○ M–Monitor and Moderate

Become aware of your ups and downs and how to control them. The more self-aware you are, the more you can control your responses. We are physical, emotional, and spiritual beings. All three areas go through highs and lows, cycles of strength and weakness. On some days, we feel stronger in one area or another. It is important to monitor or pay attention to how you feel in all three areas and make efforts to improve in the areas of weakness.

○ I–Improve Your Outlook

Research has determined that a positive outlook has physical and spiritual benefits that include the ability to fight off disease, a healthier heart, and increased resilience. When it seems that everything is against you and one thing after another is going wrong, it's important to improve your outlook. How we respond to trials often determines if we will receive the benefit of our adversity that we experience. Read James 1:2–3. When it seems that everything is against you and one thing after another is going wrong, it's important to improve your outlook. How we respond to trials often determines if we will receive the benefit of our adversity.

○ C–Gaining Control

Read Romans 6:6–23. If you experienced abuse, neglect, or family dysfunction in your early years, you encountered a loss of control. Sometimes now you may seek to control others or control your own internal stress through self-medicating, drugs, escapism, perfectionism, or in other ways. It is important to know that when you yield to God, you gain real control. Read Romans 6:6–14. You gain control by claiming God's promises. Read 2 Peter 1:3–10. You gain control by being spirit-filled. You gain control by walking in the spirit. Read Galatians 5:16.

○ Conclusion

In conclusion, I hope what you have read inspires you to be dynamic like Joseph was. Family dynamics of dysfunction can be some of the most difficult to overcome. Since you have read this far in this chapter, I'm sure the title sparked your interest as someone who has experienced family dysfunction or you know others who have. You are not alone. Research shows that six out of ten people have been affected by early household dysfunction and abuse. Sometimes we acknowledge those rough times and believe that we have gotten over them but unknowingly, our past can impact our present with negative physical and mental and spiritual health, but you can overcome your family dynamics and be dynamic.

If you want to know more about the workshops I facilitate that help you to overcome the effects of early household dysfunction and be dynamic, visit flourishandgrow.org.

Katherine L. Staten

Katherine L. Staten is a health and human service professional for well over thirty years. Her experience includes administering state and federal social service programming in local communities and working in communities that impact national research regarding evidence-based programming.

Over her thirty years of professional experience, Katherine who holds a master of science in human service counseling from National Louis University and a bachelor of science in consumer economics and family management from Southern Illinois University, has served in both public and private nonprofit organizations with a keen awareness of the real issues that families and communities face. Everywhere her influence has taken her, she always sought to advocate for the needs of people and communities. She has a wide range of experiences from providing direct services through community organizing and case management to formulating and implementing strategic plans for statewide agencies. Seeing the need to address individual, family, and community trauma, she launched Flourish and Grow to promote trauma consciousness and healing from early adversity. Her dream is for everyone to be able to approach trauma and grief and triumph over thoughts and feelings that have the potential of hindering us from bright futures to enjoy. She facilitates trainings and workshops on trauma-informed care and healing-centered engagement that translates to a social impact model to facilitate personal, organizational, and community transformation and change.

She is a certified mental health first aid instructor who allows for trainees to receive a three-year certification in mental health first aid. Her goals are to have the masses realize the pervasiveness of trauma and the symptoms of grief and loss, to the point where these topics can be discussed and addressed openly with the end result of improving the quality of life for individuals, families, and communities.

Katherine is married to retired pastor A. William Staten, Sr. The couple has five adult children and two granddaughters, Violet and Olivia.

In her book, *Descendants of Dysfunction: What we can learn from the Bible's dysfunctional families,* Katherine seeks to start conversations about family life that may be difficult. It is her hope that readers will be encouraged to move beyond pain to healing and live dynamic lives.

Connect with Katherine L. Staten on social media:
Facebook: facebook.com/KatherineLStaten
Instagram: instagram.com/Katherine_L_Staten
Visit flourishandgrow.org.

The Pearls my Family Left

ERIKA BROOKS

When I was growing up, I had the privilege of having both my mother and father in the home. We were a family of five, consisting of my parents, my older brother, myself, and my younger sister. They instilled in us a love of family, love of community, and a love of God. They were serious about us doing our homework ("getting our lesson"), learning to be and becoming good people, and having a happy childhood.

We didn't have a lot, but my parents (a stay-at-home mother and custodian father) made due. We had dinner together at the table, did grocery shopping on Friday evenings together, and watched the Friday night movie and sometimes had a sweet treat. Saturdays were cleaning days, and of course there were Saturday morning cartoons. In addition to our parents, we had our grandparents, aunts, uncles, and other extended family. And when I say extended family, you know the aunts and uncles that you are not quite sure how they are related to you but they are always around.

The ones who always had hugs and kisses for you. They always had some candy or a sweet treat for you and usually a story or joke or two. They were always happy to share a story about when they were younger, family members gone on to glory, and a life lesson for you to always remember.

I can still remember the expressions on their faces, the joy in their voices as they reminisced. I also remember sometimes thinking *What do they mean by this story?* As a child, some of the things they said or did went over my head, but as I have grown up, they make a lot of sense now. As an adult, many of these loved ones have passed away or are getting older, and I have been replaying the conversations or the movies in my head of the time spent together. I have begun to see the value of the nuggets of wisdom—whether it was words or actions—and they have really been the pearls of wisdom to be successful in my life. They are the pearls my family has given me.

Why do I call them pearls? Like a pearl, not all of the pieces of wisdom were smooth/easy to learn or live through. They were a process that took time. Some of them came from losses. Some came from heartbreak. Some came from joyous events. They also took time to form. Again, it took me years to learn some of the lessons, not a day or two. Some were harder to learn than others.

Much like pearls can be different sizes and different colors, the lessons I learned from my family were different situations, different levels of seriousness. Some of the family pearls came from the same person, many did not. Some of the pearls spoke to the same situation but were formed in slightly different ways, so they are not always identical, but they are just as meaningful. Many of the pearls they have given me are rare in that no one else had experienced what they experienced.

○ Pearl Drop: The Power of the Word No

I have always been the type of person to try and help anyone I can, and to some extent, I had been allowing it to drain me. My good friend would often get frustrated with me and tell me to stop being all things to all people. I heard her, but how could l tell people who needed me no? I tucked the words she said in my mind, and honestly, I felt bad at the thought of disappointing others and thought it to be a little selfish to say no. It was not until a child gave me this lesson that I got it. This particular Sunday after church, we were all standing around talking, and this child who may have been three years old at the time gave some of us toy flowers for Easter. She was proud of herself and her gift, and she had the biggest smile. As we talked and played with her, she reached back out for the flowers. With a chuckle, we gave them back to her, and she walked away. As she did, I asked her if I could have my flower back. She smiled and said no and continued to walk away. Now, if you have spent time with little ones, you know this is a common thing. They have no problem asking for (or taking) what they want. In that moment, I learned from this sweet, innocent child three things: 1) you are going to be told no when you least expect it, 2) ask for what I want, and more importantly, 3) *No* is a complete sentence.

It was clear sharing brought her joy—and still does to this day as she is a very loving child—but at that moment, she wanted the flower, and when I asked her for it back, she answered. She knew she wanted the flower, and that was the end of the discussion. I still remember the shock I felt—her straight, innocent face and her sense of peace as she walked away. In the moment I thought, *Why can't I do that? Why don't I ask for what I want?* Then I realized I wasn't mad or hurt that she said no to me. I realized people will be okay if I say no. They can ask others. Eventually, she came back and gave us the flowers again and let us keep them, but the lesson she gave me was worth so much more.

○ First Pearl: Family Is Everything

As I shared earlier, I have a very loving family, and there was no lack of family around. In our house, my mother and father taught us that we are all each other has and that we have to look out for one another. We were each other's first friends and continue to be that to this day. This also extended to family that technically lived outside of our home. It was nothing to have a house full at the holidays—and not just the major ones. We would have cookouts (or cook ins) for Labor Day, Fourth of July, and Easter. Easter weekend involved shopping trips on Saturday followed by an evening of getting your hair pressed for Sunday service. These weekends included aunts and cousins staying over so we could all make it on time for service in the morning. As we grew up, we were not just Aunt So-and-So's child, we were friends. We became one another's confidantes and partners in crime. We supported one another in school events, moves, and different careers. To this day, we may not see one another as often as we like, but we are still just a phone call away. This is now carrying down to the younger generations. Our support of one another does not just apply in the good times. We have had to come together in times of sickness, emergencies, and loss.

Family and "family"—those friends who should have been in your family—are some important people to have in your life. They will lift you up when you are weak. They will be your cheerleaders when you need that extra boost. They will be your light when you are struggling to see which way to go. There have been some times when I have wanted to give up and some family and friends have stood by me until I had the strength to push on. There have been times when my family has had to help with typing notes or letters, attending vendor events or online sessions to support and ease my nerves. Your family and friends will also keep you grounded and humble. They will celebrate with you but also "keep it real" with you when you are off track. Whether it is professional or personal, having a strong support system is vital.

○ Second Pearl: Trust the Process

My grandparents were wonderful people. They began working at early ages and never shied from telling us the importance of a hard day's work. They also told us to be patient and that good things come to those who wait. When you are a child, that is not necessarily what you want to hear, but you are obedient because you respect the elders. I didn't always get what they meant, but they had plenty of learning exercises for us. One such learning was working in the garden. Both of my grandfathers had gardens and loved their time in them after they finished a day's work. They would spend hours tilling the soil, planting the seeds and plants, and watering them. As children, we enjoyed going out and helping to water the plants and pulling up the crop. There is nothing like the fresh vegetables out the garden. We would then help our grandmothers with snapping the green peas or washing the greens. It could be tedious, but we did it. After we had snapped the green peas, they would cook them and then can them. (I will admit, I still do not understand the whole canning process, but they were masters at it.) Sometimes it was frustrating because we didn't get to eat them. They would tell us they were for when we really needed them. It seemed like those goodies were never going to be opened, but when it was cold and we couldn't plant anything, we were able to pop the top on the jars and have the wonderful taste of summer, whether it was green peas, stewed tomatoes, or strawberry preserves.

Another example was my mother and her craft skills. My mother used to knit, crochet, and sew. She would sew some of the prettiest dresses for my sister and me, sometimes from patterns, sometimes without. She also would create these beautiful throws through crochet. She would spend hours doing this between her work around the home and volunteering at our school. Now, I tried very hard to learn how to crochet but could never pick it up, but I did learn to knit a little. I have been able to knit small things like scarves but nothing with the fancy stitches like the pearl stitch.

I would watch her do her crocheting and sometimes grow impatient in waiting to see what it was going to be because it took so long, but she would just say, "Wait until it is finished. It is going to look nice." And she was right. When she was finished, they were beautiful multicolor throws. They were not only beautiful, they were soft, warm, and comforting when you laid under it. She could have rushed through it, but if she had, it would not have had the colors, the designs, and different crocheting techniques.

I have learned that with my work. If I take my time and hone my skills, the output is better. Sometimes when you take your time and trust the process, the finished product can be much more than you ever expected or dreamed. You may also find that the process takes you down a different path.

○ Third Pearl: Always Remember to Take Care of Yourself

My parents taught us the value of hard work, taking care of family, and taking care of community. They have always worked hard—sometimes more than one job—but found some way to relax or unwind. Living outside the country, we were afforded the opportunity to have space to ride bikes, play outside, and just be. We had space to be kids and just run around. I will be honest in saying that as I grew up and went off to college and eventually started my career, I did not do well with self-care, and some days, I still struggle, but I do try to follow what I learned. When I thought about creating a self-care routine, I often thought that I had to do something big, but my family gave so many examples of what I call "low-key ease." For example, they would take a drive or ride out with a friend. Sometimes, a quick trip on the back country road with a friend gave the space to clear the mind. Sometime the destination was to see family we hadn't talked to in a while; other times it was to get out of the house. Sometimes the trip was to run an errand, but it ended up being something totally different. I remember riding with my parents reminiscing about their past trips, hanging out, and family who had gone on.

There were the days we had some quiet time. Our parents would get us together with a game of Trouble, puzzles, checkers, or cards. We also had times in which we would all read. As I said earlier, our parents were big advocates of our education and never let us slip. They instilled a love of reading in all three of us and made sure to nurture our minds. It did not matter if we read magazines, a book, the newspaper, or the Bible. Just take some time to sit, be still, and let your mind grow. Along with my reading, I picked up a love of journaling. Both of these are techniques I continue to use to relax and unwind.

We also spent our time in church service. My parents taught us about God and made sure we had a foundation that we could build off. We often went to church but were not involved in any activities. At home, they encouraged us to pray and participated with us in prayer. This is something that continues to remain one of my biggest self-care actions. I take time to pray daily, meditate on the Word, and do good for others to fill me up.

One of the biggest self-care lessons I learned from my family was to do what you love. My mother loves being a mother and caring for others. She loves having family over, and she loves cooking, but she did do things that she wanted to do. I remember her taking her soaks in the tub, reading her books, and watching her stories (soap operas). My dad always seemed to enjoy his time outside, and he still does. He enjoys being in the yard and walking to visit neighbors. They both found their way to serve in church, which continues to feed their spirits.

◦ My Completed Pearl Necklace: Always Believe in Yourself

When I first went to college, a student in the dorm told me that I did not belong there. Not too long after that comment was made to me, an advisor told me that she did not believe I would ever graduate college, much less go on to graduate school. At eighteen, this was a huge blow to a person who was already having doubts about her abilities and about herself. When I talked with my parents about it, they told me I had just as much of a right to be there as anyone else and that they didn't make any junk. That helped me to hold my head high and continue. I eventually transferred schools and found a community where I could thrive, but that advisor's words never left my mind, nor did my parents'. All the words were there, but my parents' words were louder. I finished undergrad and continued to graduate school. I decided to write my parents' words in my planner each year to remind me they didn't make any junk.

It took me three years, but I finished graduate school with my master's degree and had a job starting the Monday after graduation. I could have chosen to believe that advisor and let her words stop me, but I chose to believe my parents and believe in myself. Was it easy? No. Did my plans go the way I thought they would? No, but I trusted the process. I refused to accept her words. Her no became my yes. I used my family for support and to cheer me on when I felt like giving up. If I had chosen to ignore the pearls of wisdom my family has given me, I would not have gotten to this place: a licensed professional counselor. The OWNER of Enlightenment Counseling Services, LLC. A writer. A podcaster.

I wear my pearls from my family proudly.

Erika Brooks

Erika Brooks is a licensed professional counselor and a certified substance abuse counselor in the state of Virginia. She received her master's of science in rehabilitation counseling from Virginia Commonwealth University. She is the owner of Enlightenment Counseling Services, LLC. Erika enjoys working with women's health issues, self-care, and trauma and grief therapy. She has been the guest on several podcasts to discuss topics around mental health and self-care, particularly in the African-American community. She will soon be releasing her podcast, *TEA Time with Erika*. Contact her at brookslpc@gmail.com, facebook.com/EnlightenmentCounselingServicesLLC, or erikabrookslpc.com.

Stepping Up and Stepping Out of Your Comfort Zone

VALARIE HARRIS

*E*xperience is the greatest teacher. I am a product of being raised in the projects but decided that the projects would not determine my destiny. Even though I experienced rejection, pain, addictions of overeating, smoking, and alcoholism along with being told I would never amount to anything, I have overcome that negativism. All those things have equipped and molded me into who I have become in this present moment. I will never feel ashamed of where I grew up. My formative years were some of the best I experienced, even with the multiple struggles. As I matured, I began to understand the importance of getting an education, which allowed me to pursue some of my dreams, passions, and desires. I also learned to depend on God as my motivational source.

Right now, I want to encourage other women leaders to put away the fear and move out by stepping up so that they can do what God has called them to do for a time such as this. I want women leaders to feel excited about walking in their purpose. Women leaders should feel good about using their gifts and talents. Their gifts will allow them to be creative, motivated, and innovative. When women are willing to put the work in to stop feeling overwhelmed, then they can confidently become ready to step up and step out of their comfort zone.

Now, my life's mission is to reach women leaders with my life message. As a female leader, I know what it feels like to be stuck. I know what it feels like not knowing how to step out of my comfort zone. I know what it feels like to be stabbed in the back by those you trust. Today, my purpose is to equip and empower women in leadership roles to lead effectively by giving them avenues that will allow them to promote self-growth through ongoing learning and to encourage them to go beyond their limitations to achieve their goals. Ultimately, I desire to help them recover from being stuck, lacking motivation and innovation to stepping up and stepping out of their comfort zone.

If you are reading this chapter right now, you will discover six pearls that can assist you in reaching your potential. They will equip you as a leader with a simple yet powerful process that will help you identify your purpose and prepare you to step up and step out. It is important to reassure women leaders that what they carry inside of them matters while encouraging them to have hope for their future dreams, passions, and visions. The Bible tells us in Psalm 37:23, "The Lord directs a person's steps, and the Lord delights in his way."

I hope that women in leadership roles will be willing to refocus on living out God's good plan for their lives. My prayer is that the impact that I will have on women leaders will be to help them walk in their purpose, pursue their dreams and visions as they encourage other women to do the same.

I struggled with stepping up and out of my comfort zone for many years, worrying about what people would think or say, but as I stepped out,

God opened doors. I am a witness that God will guide our steps as we step out in faith. That is why I am so adamant about equipping, teaching, and encouraging others by reaching out to those who need help to step up and out of their comfort zone. Think about this: What does it take to step up and step out of your comfort zone? I want to share with you six pearls that have helped me step up and step out to walk in my purpose.

○ Prayer

The first pearl to stepping up and stepping out of your comfort zone is to have a prayer life. *Merriam-Webster* dictionary defines *prayer* as an address such as a petition to God or a god in word or thought. The *Lexicon* dictionary defines prayer as a solemn request for help or expression of thanks addressed to God or an object of worship. Many scriptures have explained times when people have cried out to God, asking Him for protection, guidance, strength, healing, mercy, forgiveness, and deliverance. Prayer will enable us to step out of our comfort zone. It will give us the boldness we need. When we as leaders and entrepreneurs begin to communicate with God in prayer, it will profoundly affect our lives and those we serve. Prayer will give you a different mindset.

Roman 12:2 says, "Do not be conformed to this world, but be transformed by the renewal of your mind, that by testing you may discern what the will of God is, what is good and acceptable and perfect." As we daily renew our minds through His Word and prayer, we will be able to identify the path that God has set for us.

- Prayer brings about a growth mindset.
- Prayer will help us communicate better with others.
- Prayer will allow us to make better decisions.
- Prayer will help one to have a good attitude.
- Prayer will cause us to listen before we speak.
- Prayer will cause unity with those you work with.

- Prayer will cause us to depend on God for the answers we need.
- Prayer is the vehicle that allows us to connect to the heart of God.

As an author, coach, leadership consultant, and speaker who loves to empower, equip, and inspire others, I will always put God first in my life. Scripture tells us, God is always available to hear our petitions. Psalm 34:17 says, "When the righteous cry for help, the Lord hears and delivers them out of their troubles." Prayer is what will keep us grounded. It is our way to develop a personal relationship with God, depending on Him to help us step up and out of our comfort zone. As we submit to following God's plan for our lives, we will understand that every experience encountered in life is part of the preparation to reach our fullest potential and walk in our purpose.

○ Purpose

The second pearl to stepping up and stepping out is knowing your purpose. Ask yourself these questions:

1. Who am I?
2. Whose am I?
3. Why do I exist?
4. What is my purpose?

The word *purpose* has numerous meanings. *Merriam-Webster* dictionary defines purpose as why something is done or used and the aim, goal, or intention of something. *Vine's Expository Dictionary* defines purpose as "setting forth," "a purpose" used for God. Romans 8:28 says, "And we know that all things work together for good to those who love God, to those who are called according to His purpose." As an emerging woman leader and entrepreneur, I have learned the importance of walking in my purpose. I realized I had to keep moving forward in order to grow and become a better version of myself through the help of God.

It is imperative to understand that everyone's purpose is unique and different. As we walk in our purpose, remember that it may shift throughout your life because of the other priorities and variations of life's experiences. All of us have passions. For a few minutes, think about everything that makes you the happiest. Make a list of all the things that you love to do.

Did you know that our passions and desires come from God? Passion will drive us toward our vision, which will cause us to pursue our purpose. You can tell when someone enjoys helping others, creating things, or showing someone how to do something. Our passion will drive us toward our purpose, which will get you up early to start a new day with creative and innovative ideas. Our gifts and talents were not given to benefit ourselves but to benefit someone else. I don't know about anybody else, but I get excited about inspiring, teaching, and training others to be productive in their purpose.

Friends, we are in this thing together. We must be willing to celebrate each other's successes. Our legacy should benefit those who follow us for years and years to come. Finding your purpose sometimes can be challenging, but it is worth it. At one point in my own life, I felt lost and uncertain of my life's purpose, but what I began to realize was that I was not alone. That is why I want to leave you with some pointers on how to discover your purpose. Take note of the following statements:

1. Look within yourself.
2. Look at your past experiences.
3. Look at what you are passionate about.
4. Look at some of your past dreams God has given you over the years of your life.
5. Look at what you do well.
6. Look at the areas where you are serving others and whether you enjoy doing it.

7. Take a personality assessment (16personalities.com/free-personality-test).

8. Look at your gifts and talents.

9. If you have not taken a spiritual gifts assessment, take one (spiritualgiftstest.com/my-account-registration/).

10. Pay close attention to your inner guidance and intuition.

11. Ask for help.

○ Preparation

Preparation is the third pearl to stepping up and stepping out of your comfort zone. It is essential to understand that God has been preparing us to reach the destiny He set forth throughout our life's journey. All the struggles and various situations experienced were part of the preparation process. The Scripture is clear. Jeremiah 29:11 says, "For I know the plans I have for you," declares the Lord, "plans to prosper you and not to harm you, plans to give you hope and a future." Ultimately, He provides us with a choice to either follow our plan or follow His plan.

Things did not go so well for me when I did things my way. Every experience we have encountered in life, whether we failed or succeeded, was a teaching moment. We just had not realized what was happening. In Genesis 50:20, Joseph told His brothers, "What you meant for evil; God meant it for my good." Once you recommit to your vision, "Write the vision and make it plain on tablets, That he may run who reads it" (Habakkuk 2:2).

Our destiny has been to soar from the earth's foundation. Yes, that means from the beginning of time. Every day is practice to prepare for what we need to do on earth. Athletes practice every day to perfect their skills; that same attitude should be helpful if we want to do things with excellence. Ephesians 2:10 says, "For we are his workmanship, created in Christ Jesus for good works, which God prepared beforehand, that we should walk in them." He has already prepared us; we must believe we can

- step up
- step out on faith
- plan better
- take charge of our lives
- challenge ourselves to tackle our goals
- look for new challenges
- perform better
- think wiser
- be more confident in ourselves
- be committed
- refine ways to be creative
- believe that we can make an impact in the world
- believe that we have the power to do it

Yes, the Spirit of the Lord is upon us, but not for us alone. What the Lord has poured on us needs to be poured on the next person we can help. What we have, what we know is not for us alone; it is to be imparted into everyone else. So, as the Holy Spirit guides us to move forward in our passions and vision, we will begin to witness the provisions God has already put in place for us—the people, the finances, and other needed resources that are available.

○ Provision

Provision is the fourth pearl to stepping up and stepping out of our comfort zone. Yes, it can be very discomforting to step out of our comfort zone, not knowing our provision. Most people are content with living their lives within what's familiar. Those who are willing to take risks and push themselves beyond their comfort zones are the ones who typically achieve the most success. When I started challenging myself to do something that I was not used to doing, I exposed myself to new opportunities and experiences. If I had not stepped out, I would not have discovered all the provisions and resources available to me. I realize my capabilities are far beyond my imagination.

My friend, the same is true for you. You must speak positively about your resources and believe it. The good news is that I know that all my provisions come from God, and I have no need to worry because He is by my side. We can step out of our comfort zone with confidence, knowing that the provisions we need as we help other people will be available. He will give us the strength and courage to do what we never thought possible.

One of the provisions that we sometimes overlook is the resources that come from the relationship we have or develop with people. It is vital to understand that we have been called to serve in the Body of Christ. As we serve others, be reassured that God will provide all the resources we need to support our businesses. It is essential to rely on what the Bible tells us as leaders and entrepreneurs. Philippians 4:19 says, "And my God will supply every need of yours according to his riches in glory in Christ Jesus." He is the one that has given us the passions and dreams that lead to our purpose, and when we refocus by stepping out and stepping up, the following things will happen:

- Provisions show up.
- New doors of opportunity open.
- We begin to live with purpose.
- We begin to walk in boldness, power, and conviction.
- We begin to be a new version of ourselves.

Stepping up and stepping out can be challenging because of the unknown, but once we refocus our priorities, it will help us realign our thinking and bring balance to our lives.

○ Priority

Priority is the fifth pearl to stepping up and stepping out. Prioritizing your day is essential. It might even be worth making a schedule to ensure your life balance. Make sure you create space that will allow you to spend quality time in each area of your life. Yes, this is hard, but it can be done—your family matters. Set realistic goals that include your family, health, finances, emotional, physical, and spiritual life as you prioritize. It is crucial to set boundaries that will not interfere with your family time as a leader. Learn to say no. When you plan your schedule, please keep it simple by deciding what is the most important.

I want to leave you with this thought: God has equipped each of us with gifts and talents, and I want to use mine to help push other leaders to the point that they are ready to step up and out of their comfort zone to use their gifts to help the next person. Is it easy? No, but know that you can do it. I'm a go-getter who wants to see women leaders and entrepreneurs walk in their purpose as I equip, teach, and train them to step up and step out of their comfort zone. Have a reminder to help you stay balanced as you prioritize the essential things in life by making sure you follow some of the steps given below.

1. Prioritize by eating healthy.
   - Plan your meals.
   - Drink plenty of water.
   - Exercise.
   - Listen to your body.
   - Get an accountability partner.

2. Prioritize by renewing your body, mind, and spirit.
   - Spend time in the presence of the Lord.
   - Renew your mind daily with the washing of the Word of God.
   - Spend time praying for others as well as your own family and friends.

3. Prioritize your family obligations.
   - Spend quality time with your family.
   - Plan vacations that include going away together.
   - Communicate regularly with your family.

4. Prioritize work and ministry.
   - Do your job and ministry with excellence.
   - Never allow work or ministry to interfere with your family time.
   - Don't be afraid to say no.

5. Prioritize self-care.
   - Do something special for yourself.
   - Plan times to do your hair and nails and get a pedicure.
   - Plan times to get a massage.
   - If you feel emotional stress, there is nothing wrong with seeking a Christian counselor.

6. Prioritize having a growth mindset.
   - Never stop learning new things.
   - If you don't understand something, get help.
   - If you want to go back to school, do it.

7. Prioritize your financial obligations as a person, leader, and entrepreneur.
   - Make sure you tithe so your life and business will flourish.
   - Make sure you don't overspend.
   - Have a budget.
   - Pay off bills.
   - Invest for the future.

Unfortunately, I have had to learn some of the five pearls I shared with you the hard way throughout my life. That is why I want to share with leaders and entrepreneurs who want to step up and step out but can't understand why they can't. Things in my life distracted me from stepping up and stepping out to my fullest potential. I didn't have a prayer life until I was in trouble. Yes, I grew up in the church where I did learn how to pray, but I was not praying regularly. During some of my preparation, I made many mistakes and failed at things, but I learned to get up and dust myself off to get back to trying all over again. I often lacked the finances because I was a poor steward of what God had entrusted with me. But once I learned the principles of tithing, my life turned around. Yes, the Lord will supply all that we need, but at the same time, we must be a good steward of what He provides while at the same time helping someone else. Not prioritizing things in my life caused havoc.

So, if you are finding yourself off balance, you have not prioritized the most critical things in your life. With prayer and seeking God, "I can do all things through Christ who strengthens me" (Philippians 4:13). He is our source, and when I began to rely on Him, I was able to walk boldly, putting things in perspective, which enabled me to step up and step out of my comfort zone. Through prayer, knowing my purpose, looking at my preparation process, understanding that God is my provider, and putting my priorities in their proper perspectives in my life made all the difference.

I pray that all the pearls I shared will help bring clarity to your life as you step up and out of your comfort zone. What you have inside you matters. Stepping up and stepping out will make a difference in your life and the lives of those around you and the world.

Valarie Harris

Valarie Harris is a native of Newport News, Virginia, the only child of the late Howard and Rosa Williams. She is a wife, mother, grandmother, great-grandmother, preacher, teacher, psalmist, workshop facilitator, author, coach, leadership consultant, and speaker whose greatest desire is to seek God's face and see others in the Body of Christ grow into an intimate relationship with the living Savior. Valarie has a heart for those who desire a closer spiritual walk with God. She wants God to be glorified in everything she does.

Valarie is a retired public school teacher after devoting forty-five-plus years of her life to youth and young adults. She has earned degrees from Norfolk State University, Virginia Tech University, Liberty University, and Seraphim Ministries International Bible College. She has traveled with the Uniquely Chosen Hope Missions Team in May 2017, 2018, and 2019 for Global Missions in Ghana, West Africa, and she did workshop training in India. She has also traveled to Alaska, Puerto Rico, Amsterdam, London, Brussels, Paris, Western, and Eastern Caribbean. In May 2022, she traveled to Grenada as a part of the Project Unite Team.

Valarie is the owner of the Stepping Up and Stepping Out with Purpose Coaching & Consulting Services. As an empowerment coach, her vision is to equip, teach, train, inspire, and encourage women leaders and entrepreneurs to step up and step out of their comfort zone to reach their fullest potential. She is the author of two books. Her first book is a forty-day journal called *Talk Time with God* and her newest and second book is entitled *Unleashed Power of Prayer: Teens and Young Adults' Prayer Journal Workbook* comprised of various interactive activities. She is one of the co-authors of a new book entitled *PEARLS*.

You're Worth the Investment

PATRICIA DYER

I did not understand the importance of having a method for doing things in my life.

My mom was one of the smartest women I know. She used to say mom stuff to me when I was a kid, and I would halfway listen because being the smart worldly thirteen-year-old that I was, I surely understood life better than my mom.

How could she possibly know anything about the real world? She was a grownup and definitely did things like they did back in the olden days.

My mom had a lot of sayings. One of her favorites was, "God takes care of fools and babies."

When I would see her doing something I didn't understand and I would ask, "Why are you doing that?" she would respond, "There's a method to my madness."

I truly did not understand those pearls of wisdom my mother was sharing with me at the time about having a method.

Let's look at what the dictionary has to say. *Merriam-Webster* defines *method* as *A systematic procedure, technique, or mode of inquiry employed by or proper to a particular discipline or art, and a way, technique, or process of or for doing something.*

What my mom was trying to get me to understand was that a method is how you do things. It's the way you operate to get things done.

As a young adult, I struggled with following procedures. I felt as if they restricted my creativity. What I didn't realize then is that having a method and a plan would help me be more creative in the end. Having a plan helps you get things done.

One area that was a big struggle for me was getting up in the morning. "I'm not a morning person" is what I used to say when the alarm would ring. I would roll my eyes and suck my teeth and hit the snooze button at least once.

But the real reason I didn't like mornings was because of the sheer chaos that awaited me once I placed my feet on the floor.

How you start your day—or more specifically how you spend those first few morning hours—has a big impact on the rest of it.

I'm sure you've experienced this yourself. Have you ever had mornings where you just wanted to pull the covers back over your head and you mumbled, "I don't want to get up." Have you ever hit the snooze button and squeezed your eyes tight to catch a few more minutes of sleep? You start making bargains with yourself: "If I don't eat breakfast, I can get ten more minutes of sleep." Then you jump out of bed, and you are off to the races.

Let's be honest: When we do any of the above, we don't feel any more rested than before. Starting your day like this can leave you feeling anxious and frustrated. This is how I used to start my day. I was tired and drained before I even got out of bed.

Psalm 30:5a says, "Weeping may endure for the night but joy cometh in the morning." Why was I weeping in the morning instead of being joyful? I was like that reed being blown to and fro in the wind. I had no plans for how to have a calm and hectic-free morning, and you know what they say, "When you fail to plan, you plan to fail." No wonder I was weeping. My mornings were a big disaster. Can you relate?

Chances are that sleeping through the snooze button didn't just affect your morning but the rest of your day. You set the tone for how your day is going to go first thing in the morning.

The other day, I ran to the store to pick up a few things. By the time I finished running my errands, making two phone calls, and using the GPS, my phone died on me. Did you ever find yourself in a situation like that when your phone battery was low but you figured you have enough power to last you till you get to where you are going and before you knew it was dead?

That's the same thing that happens to us when we don't take time for ourselves in the morning to plug in to the power of God. We find ourselves trying to make it through the day on own strength, and by midday we are wore down and empty. But what would happen if we started our day by making the Savior the energy source of our morning?

What if your day started by standing on His Word, walking in His peace, and worshiping in His presence? If that happened, no matter what you faced during the day, you would be able to pull from the Lord's power and strength throughout the day.

If your mornings feel stressful and hectic, then it's time for a change.

○ How My Morning Method Revolutionized My Day

I want to share with you the process I used for making over my morning. I want to show you how you can take a few minutes in the morning to start your day in calmness and peace that will allow your mind, body, and spirit to relax and hear from God.

Think of it as a morning makeover, which will help you set the tone for your entire day. Mornings are busy, and they can be quite chaotic.

Getting yourself up and out at the start of the day can be a job. If you have a family to get ready and out the door or a pet to tend to, you know firsthand that things can go south quickly. The good news is that it doesn't have to be that way.

Earlier I shared with you how the first few hours in the morning set the tone for the entire rest of the day. Do you want that time to be rushed, frantic, and feeling like you're constantly running and trying to catch up? Or do you want it to be calm, collected, productive, and with a feeling that you're in control? It's up to you.

You do have a choice.

You can set the tone of your day. Instead of grumbling about getting up in the morning like I did, how about waking up with gratitude for another day?

○ So, Would You Like to Know What Helped Me?

I start my day with more peace, mindfulness, purpose, and clarity. Well, it all goes back to my mom's words. I needed a method to get rid of the madness I was experiencing every day. Remember, the first few hours in the morning set the tone for the rest of the day. Do you want to feel like you're constantly running behind and trying to catch up? Or do you want it to be calm, collected, productive, and have peace that you're in control? It's up to you.

Drumroll, please. I started my day by having some well-needed and well-deserved self-care.

Self-care is one of the most important things we can do for ourselves. It is so much more than getting a mani/pedi or taking a vacation. It is about understanding that you are important, and when you take care of you, it creates an environment for you to excel.

One of the most important things you can do is to create a nurturing environment for yourself so you can enjoy a peaceful start of the day. When everyone else rises for the day, you are moving in the peace and calmness that you have set.

We have been conditioned to feel that self-care is selfish. I'm here to tell you that it is not. Many also believe that self-care is a reward for dotting all the I's crossing all the T's in our lives, getting all the projects done, pressing through all the family situations, and enduring stressful times. It is not.

Self-care is one thing we need to practice for ourselves every day.

With so many things fighting for our attention (family, work, church, and business), it's easy to wind up at the end of the list. Honestly, there are times I feel like I am running on fumes. Have you ever felt like this?

I'm sure you agree that burning the candle at both ends never works long term.

As caretakers, we spend so much time taking care of others that we often neglect ourselves. Often, we get weary in well doing. The truth is that because we are not taking time out to care for ourselves, we are not truly operating in excellence.

It can be so easy for us to put ourselves at the end of our looooooong to-do list. Just like that cell phone battery, we are spent when we get to the end of the day. We don't have energy, and we wonder why.

But when you start your day with a little self-care, you will find out that you will feel better and have more energy to do all the things that you are called to do.

○ Why Do People Fail So Badly at Taking Care of Themselves?

Even when you know how important self-care is to your well-being, it isn't always easy to incorporate it into your daily routine. There are many different reasons why people fall short when it comes to practicing self-care.

One of the biggest issues is that it's often perceived as selfish. It could be you feeling guilty when you take time to focus on you. Or, you may worry what other people think or that you're a terrible person for not focusing solely on the needs of others. Let me assure you that the thought of self-care being selfish is a total myth. In fact, taking care of you helps you be a better friend, spouse, and person.

Some of the limiting beliefs I had about personal self-care were:

- I just didn't have the time to take care of me.
- When I got everything done then I'd do something for me.
- There are so many people struggling in the world, they deserved to be taken care of ahead of me.

Remember that Jesus said in John 10:10 that He has come so you can have an abundant life. An abundant life is filled with joy. It's different. It is not living in a constant state of stress-pumping adrenaline through our veins.

○ It Requires Effort

There is no getting away from the fact that self-care requires some effort on your part in the beginning. The same way you would make time in your schedule to care for others, you should set aside time to care for yourself. Caring for ourselves is the fuel we need so our light can shine bright throughout our day.

I know coming up with a self-care plan can feel like a lot of work, which is why many people put it off for another time. But understand that self-care is something you do for yourself because you are worth it. If you break down your self-care tasks into smaller tasks, it makes them much easier to implement.

Later, I'm going to share some simple things you can do today to get started on your self-care journey.

○ Different Approaches Work for Different People

Every one of us is different, which means we enjoy and dislike different things. When you initially look at examples of self-care, you'll find a lot of them relate to things like reading a book or taking a hot bubble bath. These types of activities aren't for everyone, so some people might feel self-care really isn't for them.

Self-care isn't just bubble baths, yoga, and meditation. It's things that relax you and feed your soul. So, if you find going for a run energizes you, that will become part of your self-care plan. If you find one self-care approach isn't working, try something else. Self-care should be personalized to fit your own needs.

It can be hard to get past negative thinking when it comes to practicing self-care. However, once you fully understand the importance it plays in your life, you'll find it much easier to stick to a self-care routine.

○ Ways to Practice Personal Self-care with a Busy Life

One of the most difficult challenges people face with self-care is finding the time to fit it in. When you live a busy lifestyle, it can seem almost impossible to find extra time to look after you.

So, how can you balance practicing self-care with a busy lifestyle? Here are some tips you can follow:

Schedule it in.

A good tip you can follow to ensure you can fit self-care into your busy life is to schedule it in. Think about it: You schedule in everything else you do, so why not self-care? When you set time aside to focus on yourself, you are much more likely to stick to it, no matter how busy you may be.

Establish a morning routine.

This has been a game changer in my life. I wanted to experience the joy that cometh in the morning and I was able to achieve that by creating a morning routine. I started carving out some time in my morning just for me, and my goodness, the results have been phenomenal.

During this time, I am not a mom, wife, sister, employee, or a flag and dance coach. I get to be just Pat. I sip my warm tea, look out the window, and enjoy the sun or listen to the falling rain and settle my soul. One of the most important parts of my mornings is my Christian affirmations. This allows me to start my day filled with gratitude.

○ First and Most Importantly, Your Words Have Power (Proverbs 18:21)

As soon as we open our eyes, the clock starts ticking, and all the things we would like to do, should do, and must do begin to flood our minds. When you use affirmations to start your day, they help reframe and refocus your thoughts.

The best way I have found to combat those thoughts of negativity, doubt, fear, or anxiety that show up as soon as I open my eyes is through daily affirmations. One of my favorites from *My Morning Glory* affirmation card deck is one that reads *I am well-able.*

The scripture on the affirmation card is Luke 1:37 (ESV), "For nothing is impossible with God." The prayer prompt reads, *Help me remember today that nothing is impossible with You. You have equipped me to run the race before me.*

Now that's how you start a day.

Biblical affirmations point us back to who God says we are according to the Scriptures. The next time *"must do"* shows up with the rest of the *"to do"* family and you begin to feel anxious, declare out loud, "You are well-able."

Think about it like this: Affirmations are as important to the mind as physical exercise is to the body. Speaking affirmations is a powerful way to renew your mind every day. I also love that I can carry my affirmation into my day or week. There is the power of life and death in the tongue. When I am faced with a challenge instead of responding with negative statements like "I can't" or "I won't be able to handle this," I firmly stand on what God says about me. His Word says I am well-able to and well-equipped in Him for the task that lays before me.

○ Now It's Your Turn

How can you nurture your mind, body, and soul every morning? You can be intentional.

1. ***Identify and eliminate stressful activities.*** One stressor you can avoid is reaching for your phone and scrolling the internet as soon as you wake up. You want to be careful about exposing your spirit to all that drama first thing in the morning. It won't help you start your day in peace. Watching the news can also drain your energy in the morning, so maybe add that to your day after your morning routine is finished.

2. ***Think about activities that will help create a morning that will center you.*** If you'd like to start working out more, scheduling time to exercise or go for a walk as soon as you wake up can be a great start to your day. Try playing music in the morning to get you going. When I am getting dressed, I have music playing in the house. I love how it just fills the house with worship. Try sitting on your porch or in your yard, feel the warmth of the sun on your face, and drink your coffee or tea while the family is still sleeping or before rushing to work. Try reading a book or pray and meditate. You can even try some deep breathing.

You don't have to completely overhaul your morning all at once. Instead, you can start small. Begin by taking just ten minutes out of each morning to focus on a self-care activity. Focus on developing one positive self-care habit at a time. Once you have mastered that, you can slowly add others. Starting small makes it easier to fit self-care into your busy life. Many times people make the mistake of thinking they need to begin with at least thirty minutes a day. The truth is whatever time you can free up for self-care is enough. Once you get started, you'll find it easier to focus more on your self-care due to the personal transformation you experience.

Take some time to think about how you want to create a morning routine that will help you start your day and keep you energized throughout. Make a list of three things you can start doing tomorrow to create a self-care routine that is unique to you. Keep it simple at first. You can always adjust things as you go along the way. The most important thing is to start your day from a place of serenity.

Overall, practicing self-care with a busy lifestyle may take some rearranging on your part. However, you are worth the investment. Many times when we are faced with changes in our normal routine, we tend to meet it with resistance. Instead of seeing the change as a daunting task, see it as a wonderful opportunity to revitalize your life and better yourself. Think about a pearl. It doesn't start out as a beautiful gem. Over time, the oyster takes the once annoying obstacle stuck in its shell and turns it into a precious jewel.

The tips above can help you get started on your self-care journey. Remember, self-care is essential to your health and well-being. Carving out time to nurture your body, mind, and spirit every day will put you in the right mindset to conquer the rest of your day.

Patricia Dyer

Patricia Dyer is an entrepreneur, community activist, consultant, and international speaker.

As the creative director and chief executive officer of Breakthrough Flags Ministries, her passion to praise and glorify God through dance led her to enroll and become a graduate of the Greater Allen Cathedral Genesis liturgical dance program. She received her certification and license for dance from the Dancing For Him School.

She also served as the past New York State flag sentry leader for the School of Flag Ministry.

She is blessed to say she has been involved in ministering before the Lord in dance for more than twenty-five years now, traveling throughout the United States and internationally using dance and pageantry as an evangelist tool to share the Word of God with others.

Patricia has hosted worship flag and praise dance conferences, Christian summits for servants of God, worship retreats, and workshops on the power of worship for women's ministries and churches.

Breakthrough Flags Ministries was created to present firm biblical foundations about the purpose and transformational power of flag/dance ministry.

It is her desire to help movement ministers of all abilities, shapes, sizes, and ages to develop their flag choreography and dance styles to build the Kingdom of God through movement. She does this by teaching people to develop their own unique, creative movement vocabulary so they can constantly create choreography for their ministry with ease.

She has worked alongside individuals and churches to help them create flag and dance ministries for the first time. She has also coached established flag and dance ministries to help them gain a clearer biblical understanding of what the ministry is. This helps them minister the Word of God through movement with power, purpose, and authority. As a speaker, she has been featured as a self-care expert speaking on the importance of self-care and taking care of your temple so that you can flow in excellence in your assignment.

For more information or to book Patricia for a flag conference or speaker:

Email: PatDyer@breakthroughflags.com
Website: breakthroughflags.com
Facebook: facebook.com/breakthroughflagsministries/
Instagram: instagram.com/breakthroughflagsministries/

Diamonds from Pearls

NATALIE BRYAN

To share wisdom as a woman in business initially made me nervous because I wondered what I could say to impact others. What would be the most nourishing and engaging? When I thought about writing this chapter, I felt a bit overwhelmed because I wanted my words to be different—to give the real deal not the sugar-coated stuff. I did not want to share the glamour of branded pictures and beautiful fonts, although we know how enticing and motivating they can be.

That is when I thought about diamonds and pearls in the natural. I thought about the unusual way these precious stones come into existence—one being under immense pressure and the other being created from an irritant that it needs to protect itself from. Who would have thought that these uncomfortable processes would make the most precious, beautiful stones. Have you been wondering about the title of this chapter? How do you get diamonds from pearls? You cannot naturally, but you can attain some beautiful knowledge (diamonds/gems) from pearls of wisdom. I know that some individuals may have to experience some troublesome/traumatic things to learn some difficult lessons; however, if we could bypass some of those lessons and hard experiences, then why not?

I wanted to focus on the pressure and irritants that women may face when walking into the arena of business. As women, we often face being so many things to so many people while niching out a successful business. We have seen what pressure and an irritant can produce naturally, so how does that apply to you? Why does the example of the diamond and pearl correlate to women business owners? The walk into entrepreneurship is not easy. You are facing many obstacles and a lot of pressure to produce a well-run business, no matter the issues or challenges that may arise. If successful, you will achieve a priceless objective.

What is the draw to be an entrepreneur? The ability of overseeing your own time, having freedom to work with people and on the projects as you decide, and of course the possibility of yielding the amount of money you would like to create financial freedoms. Running a business, whether large or small, can be rewarding but challenging.

As a therapist, I advocate for mental wellness daily. I would like to share some things you as a business owner or budding entrepreneur may face that may not have been considered—the mental health aspect of things that could not only impact your bottom line but literally your health.

It has been written in countless journals, articles, and blogs that female entrepreneurs can be at higher risk for mental illness due to gender obstacles, isolation, worry, and fear. Creating a maintainable work-life balance can be difficult to say the least. If we include speaking about women of color, now we also have the racial disparities that go along with the prior mentioned issues.

I want to focus on a few areas and help to identify and discuss some tools as well as coping skills that may be of assistance. I could go on and on about gender obstacles that many women in business face while being the backbone of society, and when I think about how mental illness, which could possibly be preventable, runs prevalent, I decided I should shine a light here. Life-work balance and the struggles thereof need to be taken seriously while learning to own your accomplishments. While work-life balance may be an individual thing overall, there needs to be a state of equilibrium where one can equally prioritize and maintain both the demands of work/business and your personal life.

How can this be challenging? How many nights have you laid awake completing takes, posting items for sale, or worrying about production or the bottom line? If not careful, business can consume a business owner, and they may not notice until they are well at burn-out phase.

Finances or setting unrealistic demands of oneself can consume your thoughts, emotions, and social interactions. How do we combat this? By setting boundaries:

- Set a work schedule and stick to it (not overworking).
- Say no to things that aren't on your priority list.
- Don't take on more client work when you're at your max.
- Don't overschedule yourself with calls and meetings.
- Don't constantly give free advice or show up anytime you're asked.

Create an environment that allows for flexibility. You don't have to be so rigid with yourself. There are many things that may change at a moment's notice—from schedule to availability of material to the people you network with. Being open-minded to change can help you adjust when life appears to be moving fast. Encourage team building and social interactions. As business owners, we may find ourselves being the employer or having to step outside of our comfort zones. Be open to meeting new people and engaging and collaborating in new/different arenas. You never know who may open a door for you. At times, when we carry the weight of our business, our thoughts on needs for the business, new ideas, and challenges can keep running throughout our mind endlessly.

A mental health exercise that can be helpful in this space is guided meditation. As the name implies, guided meditation allows you to be guided by someone else. A guide may help you drum up some specific mental imagery, or they may walk you through a series of breathing exercises or mantras to help you practice meditating. These services can be free or paid. These meditations can help you to be present in the moment and calm the mind. This can help to slow the blood pumping to the brain, which also slows our thought processes. This allows one to be more focused and have a clearer mind. Guided meditation helps with mindfulness, stress reduction, and relaxation.

Another issue or challenge we may face as business owners is isolation and worry. According to several business journals, the impact that loneliness has on this demographic is becoming epidemic. Statistics have stated that more than forty-five percent of business owners worry. Why is isolation such a harmful issue with business owners? Why is knowing these statistics important information for the health and wellness for business owners? Loneliness with worry has led to depression, stress, anxiety, and is one of the causes of mental illness. As business owners, we know that since this is our business, at times, we have multiple roles as the employee, the financier, the administrative assistant, and so on, and so on.

Our mental health is vital. What can we do as business owners to combat that? Start off by networking locally in your community if you feel comfortable to do so. You can even create an event for engaging work within some networking groups online. It would help to stave off the feeling of loneliness when involved with a group of people who are like-minded. Hire an employee if you can. I understand that this may not be in everyone's budget but even having a virtual assistant and interacting with them can help to reduce those feelings. Most virtual assistants can be hired at an hourly rate. Another idea that can be helpful with loneliness is finding an accountability partner. The pressure, isolation, and being overwhelmed may bring the feeling of loneliness that can be burdensome.

A coping skill that may be helpful with these feelings and emotions can be some deep breathing or grounding techniques. While both deep breathing and grounding come in many different forms of exercise, a simple grounding technique involves the five senses—the 5-4-3-2-1 method. Number five is to look. Look around for five things that you can see and say them out loud. Number four is to feel. Pay attention to your body, and think of four things you can feel. Number three is to listen. Listen for three sounds you can hear. Number two is to smell. Say two things you can smell. Lastly, number one is to taste. Say one thing you can taste. Take a deep breath and end. How did that make you feel?

Fear is real, and as a business owner, the fear of failure can be staggering. I can tell you these pictures may be polished, and these word fonts look cute, but fear held me paralyzed for a long time. Me? Yes, me. Do you know that every day I had to do it afraid and encourage myself? I am the eldest daughter of an immigrant who at one time did not have a high school diploma. I am a first-generation American, the eldest daughter to a single mother of five. I was the sacrificial lamb. I can laugh now, but looking back, it was tough. Navigating the world as the first has caused sleepless nights, worry, and stress. I said, "Why me?" a lot. Seemingly because I was the first, I was not supposed to fail. It was internalized that I did not have the option to fail.

Many who read this may be the first in their families to step out of the traditional and start a business. You may be the one to break generational curses of poverty. Crazy enough, it's not only the internal stuff that keeps us hostage. It's also the horrific expectations of others. You hear the comparisons, their opinions, and when you don't fit society's mold as successful…OMG.

I have personally heard that I am a fat, black female. I have been told I wouldn't amount to anything, I was told no one would want me, and I was told my voice would not be heard. Me the bestselling author, the owner of my own private practice, the creator of my real estate portfolio, and the owner of Cultivated Wellness, which opens doors for other entrepreneurs to get a solid start. The fear of failing is ever present; however, I have learned to do it afraid. Fear of uncertainty and rejection can be debilitating. We must stop comparing ourselves to others. In this world of the internet and social media, the falsity that has been portrayed in social media, these minuscule insights into all their successes that cause us to see very little of the failures and struggles. I have seen a creator create a four-minute video over the holidays, and it took over twenty hours to create that perfect holiday video she posted of her family, multiple takes, and several meltdowns to get the perfect four minutes. We don't always get that insight, but it's very telling how much emphasis we place on the four minutes and not the process.

One thing that I speak not only to my clients but also talk to myself about is *grace*. Allow yourself some *grace* over mistakes made or imperfections. Self-forgiveness is not only needed but necessary. This can give you that breath you need when you don't feel that there is air to breathe. Learning how to master your emotions when it comes to self-doubt can be very helpful. You can learn tools and coping techniques with a therapist or through a seasoned mentor who has been down the same road. Some things to think on to combat self-doubt:

- Don't worry about what others think.
- Set short-term goals.
- Think about your past successes.
- Surround yourself with the right people.
- Acknowledge that you're not alone.

As a BIPOC (Black, Indigenous, person of color) woman in business, our challenges can be the same in some areas and very different in others. We face biases in business in many areas, the three main ones being the lack of representation, mentorship, and funding. Understanding those challenges and engaging anyway is what we are doing every day. We must create safe spaces for us to learn and grow, not only as a business but as an individual. When we as business owners decide to move forward with our dreams, goals, and visions, let us learn to improve our chances by working on our self-development and learning how to build successful networking relationships. Let's mentor others and be open to being mentored. Let's work on ourselves daily and face possible traumas that keep us in bondage and fear. Finally, let's continue to be pearls, allowing the irritants to become our catalyst that launches us into creating something valuable, beautiful, and priceless.

I hope you received the diamonds from pearls.

> *"Your body is sacred. You're far more precious than diamonds and pearls, and you should be covered too."*
> —MUHAMMAD ALI

Natalie Bryan, LCSW

Natalie Bryan, LCSW, is a three-time bestselling author who has been devoted to serving her community and advocating for others. After completing her B.S. in interdisciplinary studies with a focus in early childhood and psychology, Natalie went on to complete her master's in social work at Adelphi University. Natalie has worked in the health and human services field for more than fifteen years, which includes experience in case management, child protective services, mental health clinical services, and working with veterans. Natalie is the owner of Restoring Harmony Counseling and Consulting, and she is also the founder of P.E.A.R.L.—Providing Education and Advocacy to Rebuild Lives—an organization that focuses on children and families in our community.

The Death of Cinderella: Let's Sort the Situation Out

LTOMAY DOUGLAS VARLACK-BUTLER

There's a difference between leading with a limp versus leading with a leak.

Leading with a limp is an outcome of fighting to overcome, and leading with a leak speaks to denying, ignoring, or depending on secular success to replace healing while causing harm along the way. It takes critical courage to let pain point to your purpose. The one way to do this is by facing your ugly truth, embracing the you that is priceless, and healing the part of you that disrupts your life as an adult. Please note, this can be triggering, so grab a cup of water and a piece of chewing gum and do box breathing if you become overwhelmed.

Poem

Does staring at the stars make me crazy
hoping to be free from this nightmare? It's hazy
Trying to remember which is more important, reading this book
Or pretending someone will show up and get me off the hook
For I feel like a fish, caught by kindness or my naiveté to trust
Dangling, suspended in torture thinking silence is a must
A must to survive like my favorite princess did because
Soon someone would discover all the abuse that was hid
Hid from the eyes of my dad, mom, and so many others
What was being done to this princess at night under the covers
Questioning my worth as I absorbed a touch that seemed to taint
Was it fantasy to long for an eraser or primer so I could paint?
I had to create a picture that I could believe
I had to find a way to breathe
It was hard as I suffocated under the cover of the daily lies
taunts that told me no one was on my side.

The dream to be like Cinderella crumbled; hope began to cave
It must be true; I'm too ugly and unworthy to save

At eight years old, my version of Cinderella died. My eyes were tainted, and the princess story of what I could one day become no longer served my innocent fascination with her fantasy. This was because I soon discovered that there was no one coming to save me. *Cinderella* was one of my favorite childhood stories. I recognized that it didn't have a perfect beginning, but what it had was a miraculous and encouraging ending. I used it to imagine a place that offered promises of love, beauty, recovery, and happiness. It gave me an escape to a place where I was the princess with a pink, pretty, frilly dress fitted around my waist, flared out, hanging to my ankles with glass slippers on my feet, and a beautiful diamond-studded tiara on my head. I took flight to an imaginary haven where magical creatures and beings would make all the ugly things disappear. It was my reset wish—the place that made me over and better. Her story became mine as I inserted my life into her world and pretended I, too, would discover the fairytale ending I longed for.

Cinderella gave me something to aspire to as I pictured myself being rescued by Prince Charming. Cinderella's story gave me hope that one day I could wake up and not have nightmares of me being violated in my bed by the babysitter. My hope in Cinderella was that her fantasy could become my real life. Interestingly enough, the Prince Charming that I was looking for wasn't necessarily a guy—I was hoping for a savior. I was looking for someone to rescue me from the heartache, disappointment, and intense fear I faced. I lived vicariously through Cinderella preparing for the ball of the century. I thought it would carry me through the difficult time I had coping with what happened to me.

I disappeared into the silence of a world that didn't exist in reality. The fairytale that I adored so much gave me a false hope and a prescription that perpetuated the maltreatment toward me. I self-medicated on misperceptions of strength and courage that I learned from fairytale moments and unrealistic expectations. I mimicked Cinderella's endurance of cruelty from her stepsisters by remaining silent, not knowing the silence was aiding the abusers. I thought I was courageous waiting for a fairy godmother to appear, despite the hell I was going through when I was really trying to put on a brave face to disguise how ugly and insignificant, I felt. As I began to think about Cinderella's story, I felt like we were kindred spirits, and maybe I shouldn't have tried to find myself in it, but as a child experiencing issues beyond my age, what else was I to do? I was conflicted and confused yet held on to a glimmer of hope that I could experience her happy ending. *Cinderella* may be a children's story, but it holds metaphors and truths that can be learned at any age. Sadly enough, it couldn't offer the solace and healing I needed. However, it can speak to the silver lining in every cloud, no matter how dark. Seeing the silver lining may appear easy, but it took some time to get clarity on why it impacted me the way it did and how it changed my perspective on life. The story told of tragedy, hardship, perseverance, and restoration. It showed how one could seemingly survive difficulty with support. My life wasn't easy, and I know that I arrived at the place I am today because of God and the people He sent who assisted me.

Cinderella's antagonists depict the meanness that springs from jealousy and how bitterness can blind one from seeing their own greatness, which in turn causes them to oppress others who are great. Jealousy added to the distress that Cinderella endured. She also unknowingly received the backlash of her stepsisters and stepmom being riddled with fear and intimidation. Cinderella's life was disrupted by the insecurities of those who were expected to care for her. Cinderella's mean stepsisters and stepmother didn't take into consideration that she was vulnerable and scared without her father. They could have nurtured her with love and comfort, but instead they loathed Cinderella.

No one thought to check in and see how I fared after my father left. I was a hurting little girl who looked to her father to affirm her. How could he affirm me when he left and I felt overlooked?

The separation of my mom and dad felt as if something had died. Maybe it was the thought that I was Daddy's girl. I was vulnerable, sensitive, impressionable, and too young to decode unspoken messages that Daddy was no longer home because things didn't work out with Mommy. No, the message I received was Daddy left home because I wasn't worth him staying around. I needed answers, clarity, and most of all, assurance that I was still loved. If Daddy was no longer there, who would tell me that I was a princess? Who would affirm that my worth was priceless?

Looking back, I can see how the mistreatment received was due to my offenders' own poor image of themselves. I'm not making an excuse for them. I just accepted that their behavior was not because of anything I did. I had to remind myself that the abuse wasn't my fault. I had come to realize that those who set out to hurt me made the choice to do so on their own. I did not encourage, seek, or ask for it. Since no one was able to explain why my daddy left and why bad things began to happen, all I could do was find some sense of solace in the fairytale book that I loved so much and wish for her happy ending.

My life was plagued with negative actions that affected my daily living. It began one night when my mom had to go to work and left me with the babysitter. It was a small three-bedroom apartment. When you walked into the apartment, the kitchen faced you. When you looked up, you could see the countless boxes of cereal lining the top of the cabinet, and to the right was a long hallway interrupted by the large living room. Farther down the hall to the left was the bedroom my sister and I slept in. Diagonally across from my bedroom was the bathroom, and around the short corner were the other two bedrooms side by side.

In reflecting on insensitive remarks regarding sexual abuse over the years, the one ignorant statement that triggered a strong reaction from me was people saying that a female "asked for" the abuse because of how she dressed. I know that statement to be so far from the truth.

The truth is I was an eight-year-old girl sleeping in her nightgown in her own bed. The babysitter had to stay over, so it never occurred to me that there was something wrong with her sleeping in the top bunk bed with me. I guess it made sense because I was the smaller child. I didn't know anything about sex—I wasn't menstruating yet—but it did not stop what happened. I was eight and in my own home, which was supposed to be a place of safety. It didn't deter the babysitter interrupting my sleep by pulling my gown up and stuffing her hand in my panties. She put her other hand over my mouth, whispered in my ear, and told me to lay still—be quiet. She continued and said if I told, she would kill me and something bad would happen to my family. I can recall thinking about the incident later in my life and blaming myself. I had strong feelings of guilt and believed it was my fault because I didn't yell. I was overcome with shame. As an eight-year-old, I believed her that if she could hurt me, surely she'd hurt my family.

So there I lay with tears coming down my face as she forced herself on me, using her finger to penetrate me. I didn't have a name for what was happening at the time, but now I know it was sexual abuse. It went on for two years.

In reflecting, I was a loner, even at the age of eight. I was different. Maybe that's why I was singled out, but after that abuse, I lived in a state of fear, confusion, and pain. I can see why I was drawn to Cinderella's plight. The story of *Cinderella* may have been age appropriate, but it wasn't realistic to the horrifying experiences I endured. It was then that the glimmer of innocence and hope disappeared. The candle that lit my heart up with dreams was blown out by the one trusted to protect me who instead abused me. It was then that I eventually gave up on the fairytale that I loved so much and declared that Cinderella died.

Cinderella and I were both princesses who daydreamed and sang while alone. She also fantasized about how things would one day get better. I, too, fantasized about how things would one day get better, and like Cinderella, I had fairies that would come around and cheer me up. Except my fairies were not furry creatures that scurried around or flew over me. Although I had real-life fairy types in my life, my experience was very different from Cinderella's. My fairies didn't show up during the day when I was home alone to rescue me or at night on the weekends when the babysitter came over. Not all of my fairies were helpful—some started out helpful and some became quite hurtful. The fairies that came into my life held titles such as teachers, leaders, church officials, and friends—even my writing pad was a type of fairy.

My fairies gave me the space to share. The thing is, I didn't tell them what I was going through. The space they gave me was one in which I could be relieved of the fear that I had to face, the secrets that tormented me, and the reality that my home no longer felt like a home. It was a safe space that they created for me that allowed me to dream for the best in spite of the horrific ordeal I was facing when I was in school, at church, or visiting with family. Initially, I lived in fear because of the threats being made to kill me if I ever told. It felt as if my silence gave the babysitter authorization to continue committing this crime against me. Sometimes she would make me stand in the corner and wouldn't let me go to the bathroom. She would prevent me from using the bathroom until I urinated on myself. It was her way of justifying touching me on my private parts because she would pretend to be so angry that she would have to wash me up. I was afraid. But what was I supposed to do?

It was like I wasn't present in those moments. I pretended I was somewhere else while the violation occurred so it wouldn't hurt as much. The whole ordeal seemed surreal. I became angry because I silently gave her consent and helplessly watched her crime of forced entry on my body. I always blamed myself because I should have told.

The truth is what was being done to me was slowly killing me. It was killing my ability to trust in adults. It was killing my ability to believe I was worth saving. It was killing my hopes that I could ever have a normal childhood. My esteem was dying. My dream of being a princess rescued by her prince was dying, and my voice being silenced was a type of death. I didn't have a clue about what was right. I knew that I didn't want to be killed, and I thought I deserved to be hurt, so I handled it the best way I could. I did what I was told. I just laid still.

In my young, undeveloped mind, doing what I was told still had to be the right thing to do, even though it hurt, right? I reconciled this to be okay because Cinderella did what she was told too. The big difference is that her dreams came true, not mine. I did what I was told. My dreams died, and the nightmares began. What was golden about the silence I kept? Wow, I wasn't even good enough like this fictional character. Even in fantasy, things didn't work out for me. Cinderella failed me. She was dead. I could barely keep hope alive, let alone Cinderella's fairytale.

No matter how much I reminded myself that her death was real, I still held on to that childish glimmer that somewhere, good was fighting to land on my doorstep. Maybe the problem with me was the fact that I relied so heavily on Cinderella's story.

Her story was inspiring—it made sense—but then reality placed a chokehold on me that almost snatched my breath away. *Cinderella is not real,* I told myself. I needed to find someone who was, someone who could be my very own fairy. So even into my adult life, I was unhealed and in search of a human to fill that fairytale void. In my adulthood, I began to volunteer in places that helped people in crisis. I served as a rape advocate, crisis counselor, and even volunteered in the church. I was so grateful anytime someone was kind to me that I happily gave of my time, talent, and gifts. It was in the church that I let my guard down and trusted that my season had arrived.

I would finally meet that person who would fill that place of emptiness that I felt, but before I go there, let's talk about the earth "fairies" that I encountered as a youth. As I spent time with my fairies, I believed that I could trust one or two with my truth. Each person that I told the truth to responded either negatively or positively. I can recall telling an adult that another adult was touching me, and they told me to shut up—I just wanted attention. They were upset that I told them the information and were visibly bothered by it. I wondered if I was wrong. Was I supposed to keep it to myself so that it didn't anger others?

I can now see how not being believed was a setup for me to be hurt again. I wonder if all children who experience pain are heard when they try to tell an adult what's happening to them. Would you listen to them with an unbiased ear and take action?

My confidence was shot. I became more vulnerable to predators who silently hide their sickness. I decided adults protected adults because children didn't have any rights. Essentially, I went through life searching for fairies to protect, heal, and celebrate me and a fairy godmother who would help my dreams manifest after first getting me to see that I was worth having them come true.

Unfortunately, I had multiple experiences similar to the negative response I mentioned. The difference is that it wasn't until I was in my thirties that I began to trust someone who appeared to have my best interests at heart. I shared with her my pain. It took many years for me to disclose my hurt, but when I did, the last thing I expected was to be hurt again.

She took the information that I shared, including my insecurity, and held me hostage to my past. She reminded me indirectly through her condescending tone and subtle comments of how tainted I was, and it made me feel less than. I figured that she knew best because she was a woman who served God, was faithful to her husband, and a leader in the church. I wanted to be like her. I looked up to her. I thought she would be the one to restore me to whom God says I am.

It didn't quite work out that way. She saw the potential and the talents, but only used them for her benefit. She didn't cultivate the gifts that I have, nor did she affirm how precious I am. Speaking in terms of development, others can help cultivate our gifts through guidance and positive feedback. She was supposed to be my mentor—or like in Cinderella's case, my fairy godmother. The truth is, she was more like the evil stepmother in the story because she kept me in a box, stagnated and blinded to the greatness that not only is present within me, but that lay ahead of me. I would often find out how she told my personal information to others, which caused many to whisper behind my back. I became withdrawn and isolated because I was crushed knowing that someone I held in such high esteem would make me feel so low. No one gave me permission to admit out loud that I needed healing.

In the story of *Cinderella,* the people who lived on the outside didn't know what was really happening behind closed doors. Her life may have appeared to be good to those who observed from the outside, especially because she was living in a beautiful home, but they didn't see how her stepmother was mistreating her and how cruel her stepsisters were. Sadly, that is usually the case. Society, neighbors, friends, and family sometimes don't discover what's happening until it's too late.

I didn't have a stepmother nor stepsisters, but there were things happening behind closed doors that no one knew about. It's those things that happen that can delay a dream, stop progress, and cause one to feel as if all hope is gone. It's those things hidden behind closed doors and sealed with silence that can corner you into a state of isolation. A word that comes to mind that can describe what happens in isolation is *suffocation*. When I was living with secrets that hurt, it made me feel that my voice no longer mattered, so I remained quiet.

The silence became a self-made prison. It dictated my actions and guarded my words. I didn't know how much the silence would allow the hopes, dreams, and life to slowly seep out of me. How can you hold on to a dream that you will one day be someone great when you are constantly treated like you are the least? How can you continue to sing when it feels like your voice doesn't matter? How do you tell others what's really going on when everyone thinks you have the perfect life, or they simply think you're a foolish child talking too much?

Cinderella was a story that made easing the pain appear easy. I kept fooling myself into thinking that all I have to do is something else—anything else—to take my mind off what was happening. I wanted to be just like Cinderella and pretend my pain away. She would sweep, swirl, talk to the squirrels, laugh, and have fun, all while getting her stepmom's housework done. Can I tell you of the days that I really dreamed, fantasized, and wished that I could jump into my *Cinderella* book and be her? I wished I had two mean stepsisters and an evil stepmom who made me do housework. The sad thing is that all I had was a *Cinderella* book as a self-help guide on how to handle life, and my life looked nothing like hers, yet I believed all pain was the same.

Not true.

Quite honestly, I was too young to know that certain things should not be kept a secret. No one told me what was appropriate for an eight-year-old to endure. Didn't I have a right to be informed about the difference between touching in the safe zones versus the danger zones? I get that adults would like to think, *Not my kid* or *It won't happen in my family*, but it doesn't mean that a child should not be taught anyway. As a child, no one seemed to think that I had any rights. No one gave me the right to be heard, and my right to be safe was disgraced. I learned to somewhat cope by matching my storyline with Cinderella's, trying to outlast the terror with stories of happily ever after.

I was only eight, and when adult things happen to you at that age, it's no wonder that the lines become blurred. It was as if my happy ending was trapped inside of a snow globe, and then suddenly the shaking began, which was synonymous with the abuse and fluttered my vision of peace with a snowfall of pieces of me falling from the once calm and safe scenery. I didn't realize that I was numbing my pain by using Cinderella's story as a coping mechanism. I thought that day in and day out, this beautiful princess who was subjected to cruelty, condescending words, and hard work was admirable because she didn't allow the injustice to change her character.

Cinderella remained optimistic, kind to those who mistreated her, and hopeful. I deceived myself into believing that I had to be cordial to those who abused me. I caused more injury to myself by not knowing the proper way to deal with what was going on in my childhood. I reckoned that that was the one thing missing from Cinderella's story, her process. The story of Cinderella moves the reader through a sequence of events that shows how she went from pity to the palace. I don't recall the story sharing how Cinderella was depressed, angry, not wanting to eat, thinking that life would be better without her, and if she experienced any of those feelings, there was no explanation of how she made it through. I mean, she did have a fairy godmother who showed up when she was very sad about being unable to go to the ball, but even with that, the story doesn't give an account of how she was impacted and what she did to overcome. It was an unrealistic expectation that I had as a little girl to think that my life issues would be solved by simply wishing I was someone who only existed in fiction. What can I say? My *Cinderella* book was the kind of dialogue I craved, but it wasn't the conversation needed to change my situation.

Cinderella didn't help me to understand that I needed more than fairies and a smile on my face to make it through. It didn't teach me how to really see a happy ending. Clearly, the children's story is timeless, and the actual character is still alive in fantasy land. However, the beauty and all that *Cinderella* stood for became nonexistent to me. It came to a point in my heart that I could no longer believe in a happy ending. How could an eight-year-old keep cleaning up the mess of those entrusted to care for her when her hope was fading daily? My mind was too young to compute that a happy ending was possible when I was trapped in an unhappy beginning.

Not even her magic could help me. I felt like the only relief was not waking up from my sleep. I mean after all, it wasn't a dream I lived, but a nightmare I faced when it was time to climb in my top bunk bed. My nights were filled with dread. It was crucial to experience the rescue, for without it, I was forced to lay still and play dead. I did, however, acquire new skills. I learned to pretend, shut down, and beat my mind into submission and tell my brain to make me numb to the pain that was screaming that I deserved to be abused and used, that I was worthless and not worth an adult hearing my truth. I told my brain to numb the reality that with every touch, the force of her hand would soon stop, and maybe she would be satisfied. What did I do to cause this piercing of my heart? There was a slow leak in my heart. I was losing hope. Trust was torn, and the sheer delight of being saved was long gone. I accepted defeat, and any act of kindness shown to me was a treat. I learned how to look people in the face and lie because I caved in to fear and gave her the answer of "no" when the question, "Are you going to tell?" was asked.

So, of course, I soon developed the ability to wear a fictional mask. My true face no one could see because the truth is I didn't think others thought I was worthy of breathing, and that's why I lived out this untruth, that my body only had one use.

This is my journey still in progress because healing is like learning, and we do it every day. If you bypass doing your inner work, you will run the risk of being influenced by your unhealed part. Leaders who know, love, and embrace themselves learn from, care for, and show compassion for those they lead. To lead without knowing oneself is like the blind leading the blind. How can you equitably and responsibly manage others when you won't manage you? When two unhealed people have conflict, it's usually their inner child showing up interacting with one another.

It's why I offer **PEARL** as a five-step framework to sort the situation out. *Process* your pain, *Examine* your beliefs about self and others, *Appreciate* the path and strengths held, *Reflect* on the outcomes of your engagement with others, and *Learn the lessons* and love yourself.

○ Reflection Questions

1. If someone shared their story about their truth with you, how do you think you would handle the situation? Would you become uncomfortable and end the discussion, or would you lean in and listen?
2. Identify a time where you tried to fill a void in your life.
3. Why is it hard to disclose harm experienced as a child/adult?
4. As you self-reflect, are you leading with a limp or with a leak? Why did you decide on your answer?

You can find a continuation of my story in my upcoming book, Tamar's Truth.

LTomay Douglas Varlack-Butler, MSW, CASACT

LTomay Douglas Varlack-Butler, a PhD student in education for social justice at the University of San Diego, is a resident practitioner and part of the national training team in the Center for Restorative Justice. She is a social worker, substance abuse counselor, and a Restorative Roots collaborative member facilitating Participatory Action Research.

Tomay integrates her mediation, mindfulness, and trauma training into her work where she provides conflict coaching, family conferencing, anti-racism work, and healing circles for persons who've experienced trauma. Her commitments to social justice and transforming lives deepen her practice and commitment to living a restorative lifestyle. Tomay's work as a facilitator and trainer includes working in higher ed, K–12, community agencies, and religious organizations.

Tomay is the proud mom of two college graduates, loves to write and sing, and in her free time, produces two media projects—*Unbranded Talk Show* and the *Worth Justice Network*. Learn more at brandmebeautifulinc.com.

Beautiful, Brilliant, and Broken

CARMEN JIMENEZ-PRIDE

On my worst days, I put on a pair of dramatic lashes and a lip color not in my daily lineup, and I feel a little bit better when I step out into the world. There is something about a full face of makeup, flashy accessories, and a nice handbag that can shift an entire mood. The power of waterproof mascara and setting spray can lock a full face of makeup, which becomes resistant to tears. It is not about being someone I am not but more about attempting to hide the pain in environments where I do not feel safe to show my tears or safe to show up expressing my pain. Walking around in a woman's body—a black woman's body—history has given us many lessons telling us we must be strong, resistant, and have the ability to take on the world at any given moment. But what about the days that feel impossible to show up and I still have to be all the things? I put on my full face, grab my bag, and step into the world because I am beautiful, brilliant, and broken.

While taking a thirteen-hour drive, which should have been nine hours, due to random stops to sightsee, I had the goal of surprising my mother for her birthday. While traveling and in a full nineties R&B and rap Jeep concert, featuring yours truly as lead and background singer, I got a phone call from the president and chief executive officer of the Association for Play Therapy informing me that I was nominated by multiple peers and awarded the 2021 Emerging Leader Award, and I would be honored at the International Play Therapy Association conference. I had to pull over for one of those random stops to get myself together because I was in tears due to knowing multiple peers nominated me and the fact that I actually was awarded.

Over the last three years, I have been *Braving the Wilderness,* which is an amazing book by Dr. Brené Brown focusing on the courage to stand alone and the quest for true belonging. In her teaching, she shares that belonging is not about fitting in, being someone you are not, and making the people around you feel comfortable but more focused on being vulnerable, being uncomfortable, and being around others without presenting like someone you are not and taking ownership of your values.

I made a decision prior to that to step out of my comfort zone to change the trajectory of the field of play therapy with more focus on culture and diversity. I also made a goal to increase my visibility to the public by building my platform on and off social media. I made a commitment to myself to share my knowledge with others by increasing the amount of training I host and speaking engagements I said yes to along with a goal to turn my love for tea and herbs into a business that would make my ancestors proud. As a serial entrepreneur with multiple businesses and really big goals and dreams, there was a need to focus on how growing professionally can affect me personally and mentally.

As a clinical mental health professional within my practice, I utilize a therapeutic model called Internal Family Systems (IFS). This approach to psychotherapy identifies and addresses multiple subpersonalities, which we call "parts" within a person's mental system. As the therapist, I assist people with connecting to their parts, building a relationship with them, and assisting with the healing of traumatized parts. Not only do I offer this therapeutic approach to my psychotherapy clients, I also offer it to my business coaching clients. Most importantly, I utilize this model within my personal mental health journey. Yes, I said it: my personal mental health journey—I am a therapist with a therapist. I believe in healing the healer.

To be completely transparent, I suffer from anxiety disorder and have experienced childhood trauma. In IFS terms, I have broken child parts within my internal system. Becoming a mental health professional motivated me to take the time to do my own personal work. I firmly believe that if we do not address our childhood trauma and our traumatizing adult experiences, they will continue to show up and impact our choices and decisions. Utilizing the IFS model helps me understand I am not my trauma, I am not those childhood experiences, and I do not have to be a direct reflection of the choices and decisions of my parents.

I have learned that I can make poor decisions, learn from them, and do things differently.

I have learned that I can make mistakes, forgive myself, and move forward.

I have learned to forgive myself and others.

I have learned to ask for forgiveness.

I have learned to apologize to my parts (myself) and others.

I have learned that unaddressed mental health issues can have a major impact on your business—how the business is started, the foundations of the business, and the growth of the business.

○ Business and Mental Health

When I conduct business coaching, during the first session, I discuss the IFS concepts and give my client the homework of evaluating their business to see how traumatic experiences have impacted their business choices. Often, the client is able to connect business behaviors to past experiences.

When this is evaluated, the client begins to recognize and discuss a connection between their mental health, choices, personal values, and morals to their businesses.

Why is this important? There is a connection between our personal lives and our business lives. There is a connection between our childhood relationship experiences and our adult relationship experiences. When in adult situations, parts of you may not know how to handle the interaction and will resort to behaviors of protection, and these behaviors can appear child-like. While in the professional arena and even in some personal spaces, these can be damaging behaviors that can have a lasting impact on relationships and decisions.

You can be beautiful, brilliant, and broken, but acknowledging the brokenness—giving it the attention it needs—is key.

Beautiful

Having qualities of beauty
Exciting aesthetic pleasure
Generally pleasing

Beauty is only skin deep was a phrase I would hear often growing up. In my opinion, beauty is more than someone's looks. Beauty can include someone's character. The mental and moral qualities of a person can impact their business and how they show up in not only the professional arena, but also a personal arena. A lot of professions operate with a code of ethics, standards, or other guidelines that outline methods of conduct in the professional world. When looking from a personal perspective, someone's values and morals can be considered their code of conduct. With a lack of emotional awareness of how personal issues can affect professional choices and professional relationships, an individual can put themselves at risk of losing their integrity and allowing their child-like parts to take center stage.

Brilliant

Very bright
Striking, distinctive
Distinguished by unusual mental keenness or alertness

Brilliance can mean different things to a person. Brilliance can be a developed skillset. Brilliance can be measured by someone's level of education. Brilliance can be how someone navigates the world. Our life experiences are how we measure brilliance. Others will see a level of brilliance within us that we do not see, and this can be based on our personal views of ourselves. Others may have a level of brilliance that the world does not see or acknowledge. Doing personal work will increase the ability to see yourself and take ownership of who you are, the skillset that you have, and how you show up in the world.

Broken

Damaged or altered by or as if by breaking
Not working properly
Made weak or infirm

Our life experiences do not have to define who we are. Our life experiences do not have to impact our personal and professional lives. This can only happen when we acknowledge our trauma and situations of the past.

I present with past trauma and past poor decisions. I have learned a lot of lessons from those experiences. I firmly believe that I am proof of not allowing the past to have full control of my present and future. This is why it is important to do the work and take notes from the lessons learned to move forward to reaching your goals and dreams.

Carmen Jimenez-Pride, LCSW

For Carmen Jimenez-Pride, LCSW, therapy is her lifeline. She's not just your typical therapist. Her skillset extends from clinical outpatient services to coaching, with many other products and services in between. Making your mental health a priority is a big step, and she acknowledges that. She fully believes that your mental health journey is more than a service; it's an experience—a transformative experience where we connect and grow together. If you're wondering if she's qualified, the real question is how qualified is she. Carmen is a licensed clinical social worker in Georgia and North Carolina, licensed independent social worker clinical practice in South Carolina, registered play therapist, and substance abuse professional. She has provided clinical outpatient therapy as well as intensive in-home services. In 2011, she opened Outspoken Counseling and Consulting to provide therapy, life coaching, and business consulting. In 2020, she created Diversity in Play Therapy, with the mission to affect change within the practice of play therapy by increasing cultural awareness and cultural competence for healers working with diverse populations. She has also hosted the Diversity in Play Therapy Summit. Over the years, she has definitely embodied and lived the motto: "I grow, you grow, together we will grow."

Website: carmenpride.com
Email: carmen@outspokenllc.com

Positioning, Visibility, and Authority

SHARVETTE MITCHELL

*Q*ueen Elizabeth II and I have something in common—sorta kinda.

Let me explain.

I am an accessories kind of girl. If you look at any of my pictures on social media or on my website, you will see that I wear accessories. Whether that is statement jewelry from Sassy Jones Boutique or luxury jewelry from David Yurman, I always have something on.

My first statement necklace, which I wore to death, was a multi-strand pewter-gray pearl necklace I purchased from Dell Scott of Divacoutoure in 2011. The necklace was not made of real pearls, but it was something about the multi-strands that I just loved. I always felt elegant and in charge with that necklace. As a plus-size sister, I figured out that you need bold and powerful jewelry to match your big and grand presence.

I have certainly added to my statement jewelry collection since then, but that necklace still finds a special place in my heart and around my neck every now and again.

Now…back to Queen Elizabeth II.

According to The Royal Family Channel, Queen Elizabeth II is rarely seen in public without her favorite three-strand pearl necklace—a gift from her beloved father, King George VI, who passed away in 1952.

The future monarch at the time was only twenty-five years old when she lost her dad, and the pearl necklace that she received from him as a young girl remains a powerful reminder of the special bond they shared.

Queen Elizabeth loved the necklace so much that she had an identical one made, and in 1953, a third three-stand pearl necklace joined her collection.

For the past seventy-plus years, Great Britain's longest-reigning monarch has incorporated the three-strand pearl necklaces into her "official uniform."

So Queen Elizabeth II and I both love multi-strand pearl necklaces.

I started thinking about the advice I wanted to share with entrepreneurs and business owners who will read this book collaboration, and it jumped out at me that there are three things (like the three-strand pearl necklaces that Queen Elizabeth and I like to wear) that help grow, expand, and market someone's personal brand and platform. They are positioning, visibility, and authority.

In particular, this conversation is for those of you who are professional service providers, leaders, experts, nonprofit leaders, and ministry leaders. Let me remind you that *you* are the brand. Whether you are a therapist, accountant, lawyer, real estate agent, life coach, or financial counselor, your intellectual property and your experiences translate into a product. Furthermore, potential customers are deciding to do business with you or your firm because of your personal brand. This chapter is about elevating and building the positioning, visibility, and authority of that brand.

But before we jump in…

Who is your target audience, ideal client, or avatar?

Sometimes I ask this question and people say, "Well, everyone could use my service" or "Everyone could use my product."

Insert spoiler alert: Your target audience is not everyone. Your business and your brand should have a specific aim and a specific focus related to *who* you are here to serve and who your product or services are best suited for. If you've ever played darts, then you're probably aware you're trying to hit a target. We are always aiming for the center, right? Why?

Because you must have some type of focus.

It's the same way with your target audience for your products and services. That customer or person could be just a figure in your head right now, but let's drill down where we want to start. When thinking about identifying and honing in on our target audience, first look at people who have the pain points and problems that your service solves. What are the problems they are having? What problem does your product or service solve? I literally want you to put this book down and write that answer out.

Every single product or service solves a problem, need, or want.

You might think, *I just sell T-shirts.* That's not really a problem. We have to wear clothes, right? We can't walk around without clothes on, so a pain point could be as simple as that.

I heard business strategist Danielle Jarvey Harmon say that people who are in pain are actively looking for a painkiller. Let me say that again: *People who are in pain are actively looking for a painkiller.* Your marketing message and marketing process can call out these pain points or problems and highlight *your* business as the solution, and as a reminder, your service or your product is a solution. It's a solution to somebody's pain point. It's a solution to somebody's problem. It is a solution.

So let's walk through some questions you can start asking yourself related to your target audience. This will help you get more clear and honed in on the customers you really want to go after and who you really want to serve with your business.

How would you describe your ideal client? What do you think about them when you see them in your mind? What's their buying behavior? For example, a typical Walmart shopper is probably very price sensitive. They're looking for the lowest price or bulk purchase, so the buying behavior of your ideal client is something that you want to think about. Is this person an impulse buyer, or is he or she more of a processor who needs a lot of information before making a buying decision? What does this look like for your target audience?

Are they high-end shoppers who like Neiman Marcus, Bloomingdale's, and boutiques? Are they grocery shopping at Food Lion, or are they going to Whole Foods? Where are they shopping?

Begin to formulate and think about these descriptors for your target audience. What type of TV shows do they watch? Do they even watch TV?

I heard someone describe a conversation that was had with the owner of Rolls Royce, and they asked him, "Why don't we ever see TV commercials for Rolls Royces?"

The owner of Rolls Royce replied, "Because my audience doesn't watch TV."

Everything will improve related to your marketing and your sales process as you get clearer about your avatar and target audience. Oh, and heads up: Your avatar and your target audience may evolve as you evolve as a business owner and as your brand evolves. And in addition, you will find that it will become easier to find your target audience when you know who you're looking for, and it will become easier to present to them the solutions that you have related to the problems that they are experiencing. This will help move them to action, which is purchasing your services and doing business with you, and that's a good thing.

Now that we are more clear on *who* we want to attract, let's get into positioning, visibility, and authority in your marketing. This is our three-strand pearl necklace for your business. Let me define each from the standard definition that you find in *Merriam-Webster* and also the marketing definition for our purposes.

○ Pearl Strand One: Positioning

Positioning is defined by *Merriam-Webster* as to put or arrange someone or something in a particular place or way. Positioning from a marketing standpoint refers to the place that a brand occupies in the mind of the customer and how it is distinguished from the products and services of the competitors.

○ Pearl Strand Two: Visibility

Visibility is defined by *Merriam-Webster* as the state of being able to see or be seen. Visibility from a marketing standpoint means using multiple methods to reach your customers rather than just one or two ways but includes both online and offline communication. In addition, brand awareness is the extent to which consumers can recognize or remember a particular brand.

○ Pearl Strand Three: Authority

Authority, defined by *Merriam-Webster,* is the power to influence or command thought, opinion, or behavior. Authority from the marketing standpoint refers to using your experience and knowledge to establish yourself as a trusted source or an expert in your field.

Before I give you advice on building and growing your positioning, visibility, and authority, let me address some potential questions or statements that may be coming up in your mind.

Some of you might be reading this and saying, "I'm an introvert. I want to stay behind the scenes. I want to stay behind my brand and my product." So this conversation around building visibility, positioning, and authority may feel scary to you. I acknowledge that feeling, however, here's a question I want to ask you: Is your fear of the spotlight keeping your business invisible? I want you to think about that.

Some of you might be saying to yourself, "Well, my competitors or other service providers are better than me. Their products are better than mine. It looks like they're getting more customers than me, and I just feel like they're doing better." My question to you is, are they better, or do they market better or have a better mindset?

Lastly, some of you might feel like you are standing still but spinning in circles all at the same time when it comes to promoting your business, your brand, and your organization. My question to you is, have you looked at what you're doing, and do you have a trusted guide? My hope is that the rest of this chapter will be a trusted guide for you to start these conversations of gaining positioning, visibility, and authority for your business and for your brand. The world is waiting for you.

○ Pearl Strand One: Positioning

Let's talk about the first strand of pearls, which is positioning. As a reminder, positioning refers to the place that a brand occupies in the mind of the customers and how it is distinguished from the products and services of the competitor. Imagine your potential ideal customer has a list of options for certain products and services. Imagine that they have a notebook or journal in front of them and they have jotted down potential options for services or products that you provide. Is your company, brand, or name on that list?

And how high up on the list are you? That's positioning.

Your first question may be, "How do I get on this list?"

Well, we start with your core offering. What is it that you actually offer to the world? What are your services? What are the options? What are the ways that people can work with you? What are the types of products that you have? What are the results you promise to customers?

You want to make sure that you're crystal clear about what you are actually offering to the world because that's going to help with positioning you in front of the types of customers you want to have. Remember those avatars that we talked about a few pages back? Your service offerings and your products should appeal to your avatar or ideal client, and they should be something that is a solution for them.

The next thing that's critically important to positioning your brand in front of your ideal client is all about your pricing, which should reflect the value that your product or service brings to the table. For professional service providers, your price should consider the results or transformation that the customer can expect. If your ideal client is price sensitive, you will need to factor that into your pricing and look for the most efficient way to provide your service or product to keep costs down. On the flip side, if your ideal client is not price sensitive and sees the value in quality services, pricing too low may tell them that your value is low. You can do marketing research for pricing information and general pricing structure for your industry, however, it really comes down to the promise that your brand delivers.

Now let's talk about one of my favorite topics: visual branding, which can position your brand and put you on the list higher than your competitors. What is it that customers can *see* that represents your brand? Let me remind you that people make an assessment about what your company and your brand bring to the table simply based off what they see. That's all that they have initially, that's before they learn about your amazing services, before they hear your brand stories, before they read testimonials. Customers are going to make an assessment and an assumption based off how you show up visually. Are you visually appealing to your customers?

Let's talk about what I mean by visual branding. This includes your brand photography—headshots, as well as photos used to represent your business on social media, your website, your blog, in your email marketing, and any type of product photos. All of those must be top notch so that the photography pulls in your ideal client and showcases that you are the option they should select.

Your visual branding also has to do with your brand colors. Are you utilizing a consistent color scheme? You should have two to five core colors you are using all of the time. Your brand colors for your online marketing and for your offline marketing should be the same. They should be consistent across your website, business cards, brochures, flyers, packaging, signage, banners, social media, graphics, emails, postcard marketing, etc.

And even though it seems like a simple thing, just having the consistency of brand colors helps with the recognition of your brand for a lot of customers. What we want is for your ideal clients to recognize you and to have you at the top of their options on their list. So your visual branding is incredibly important. Sometimes people say that visual branding is not important, but quite honestly, you don't want it to distract from what you bring to the table—and that's online and offline—so, work on ensuring that you have great graphics, great visuals, and that you're using consistent brand colors that will help position your brand and put you at the top of your potential customers' list of options.

Now that we have talked about positioning, let's talk about the second strand of our three-strand pearl necklace, visibility.

○ Pearl Strand Two: Visibility

As a reminder, visibility means using multiple methods to reach your customers rather than just one or two, including both online and offline. Visibility is about the voice of your brand and how you communicate that to the world. How is your target audience able to experience the voice of your brand? How can potential customers experience the story of your brand and your brand promise? The short answer is that we have to be where they are and get in front of them.

Here are some of the top visibility strategies that you can execute for your business: social media marketing, email marketing, speaking, and events.

Visibility Strategy—Social Media

For those of you that are professional service providers, keep in mind that your visibility is incredibly important on social media, which is the front door. It is now really where first impressions are happening and where first impressions are being made. Many times people are referring business to you, and people are going to look you up on social media. What do they see when they find you?

So, if you're questioning whether you should be on social media, the answer is absolutely…yes. Now what you must determine is where your avatar or ideal client is hanging out on social media, and then you want to go and show up there. You don't need to be on all five hundred social media sites. All jokes aside! There might not be five hundred, but there are a lot. The key is to determine where referrals are coming from and where your ideal clients like to be.

Social media can be a funnel to grab leads and customers. It's really the top of the funnel. We leverage social media so that we can get introduced to potential customers and get visibility with them for the sake of funneling them into our space on the web, which is our main website, or funneling them into a consultation or email list. When we're building visibility, we also want to leverage social media and use social media to showcase the story of the brand and the behind the scenes of the brand. We also want to talk about customer testimonials, in addition to wins and recognition that our company has received. So as a recap: Leverage social media to communicate what your brand has to offer, showcase your expertise, build leads, and get customers.

Visibility Strategy—Email Marketing

A lot of times people feel like social media is the end all be all; however, you want to also leverage email marketing. When we think about visibility, which is about communicating with potential customers, what are all the ways that we can stay top of mind with customers? Email marketing is one of the most direct forms of communication, so it's a visibility activity that you want to do. I bet if you checked your phone *right now*, some of your favorite brands and stores have sent you a few emails in the last week. Some stores send emails every day.

The first thing that we have to do is actually capture email addresses.

Often you will need a lead magnet or what's called an opt-in that entices potential customers to give over their email address in exchange for something of value. That may be a coupon code, a checklist, entry into a free webinar, et cetera. So, the first step of email marketing is determining how your brand and business want to actually ask for and capture the email addresses. You will need an email marketing tool for this such as GetResponse, MailerLite, Active Campaign, Keep, et cetera.

The second step of email marketing is nurturing your list. Now, I got to say, a lot of small businesses do a good job of the first step. They will capture the email addresses, but they fall short in actually continuing to communicate and nurture the relationships. You want to think about the email address as a person, and that is the relationship that you're nurturing. Not only do you capture their email, but you also want to talk to them by way of sending out frequent emails. My guidance is one to four times per month when you're not in a launch phase.

There are lots of things that you can share in an email to clients: give tips; answer frequently asked questions; share industry news and video links; and certainly sell your products and services. You can also showcase customers and testimonials or talk about your speaking engagements, events, and anything notable that's going on with your business. Leverage that time to build your relationship with your email list and most importantly stay visible, and that's going to drive sales.

As a reminder, there are people who are eight years old and eighty years old who all have email addresses, so your avatar and your ideal client are checking their email probably every single day, if not multiple times a day. You want one of your visibility activities to be email marketing to stay in the top of their mind as a resource and a potential option for products and services.

Visibility Strategy—Speaking

The next visibility activity that I'm going to recommend is speaking. Yes, I want you to seek and create speaking opportunities. Literally every business owner can speak about their area of expertise, their products, how they do business, the benefits of their product, et cetera.

There are organizations, conferences, symposiums, and seminars that are looking for speakers who are experts. What's so beautiful about speaking and having speaking engagements is that it allows for a two-way communication. Sometimes social media might feel like a one-way communication. Email marketing may even feel like a one-way communication. But when you have the opportunity to speak, whether that's virtual or in person, you have the instant ability to build rapport, answer questions, and talk directly to potential customers. For professional service providers, nothing else really matches that.

Speaking also allows you to continue building your audience. We all know that one of our business goals is to continue to get in front of our ideal client and our avatar. When you speak at someone's event, they have curated this audience that now you get access to. You have the ability to build on to your audience by meeting these new people while you show up as the expert and leader that you are.

Converting someone to a customer is always easiest when you're in person. That's why speaking and becoming a speaker are powerful options for business owners because you have the ability to be directly there with people who are potential customers who can turn into actual customers just because they saw you speak. Oh, and you can grow your email list and social media following as well.

Visibility Strategy—Events

Hosting events, big or small, is a great visibility strategy. Yes, I'm referring to *you* actually hosting your own events. One of the great things about events is that you get to really show up as a leader, and leaders get paid more.

When we think about all of the ways we can get in front of customers, live events is absolutely one of the things you want to put on your radar.

This doesn't have to be a big, grand three-to-five-day conference. This could be a local meetup, a local networking, or cocktail hour or small workshop. This could be an online webinar, conference, summit, or teleseminar. When you host and promote an event, it shows you and your business in a leadership spotlight. It also has an interesting tribe effect that I like to refer to because your customers now get to gather in this space that you've created. And again, whether that's online or offline, potential customers get together, and they get to network and connect with each other, and they attribute that all to you and to your event.

To date, I have hosted (in person) six conferences, a retreat, a workshop, and a luncheon. I have to say that hosting my events was one of the things that changed the trajectory of my business and visibility. There are people who will come to an event first before they buy a service. They will be attracted to your event. Also, with the marketing of events, that draws attention and different attraction to your company and your business. Certainly you can generate revenue with events. So that's another benefit of including events as a visibility activity for your business.

In summary, these are the main visibility activities I recommend you work on for your personal brand and business. Let's chat about the last strand of our three-strand pearl necklace.

○ Pearl Strand Three: Authority

Authority marketing refers to using your experience and knowledge to establish yourself as a trusted source and an expert in your field. Authority in marketing really is about your spoken or written intellectual property and expertise. So how do we showcase your intellectual property?

As a business owner, you are an expert in something or some field. Media is looking for experts. They want people who have intellectual property. They want people who have valid opinions they can share with their audience. In addition, it's kind of cool to be featured in media. I love what Adam Witty said in his book *Authority Marketing*: You actually want a little bit of a celebrity factor on your business and brand. You want people to feel like, *Oh, I get to work with so and so* or *I get to be their client.* Media exposure can give you that celebrity factor.

For the media outlet that features you, their brand and their visibility get attached to you. That's why you want to be seeking media opportunities. In addition, it puts you in front of new audiences. That media outlet has an audience that you don't have access to, but now you will have access to them.

But here's the other thing that you can do to establish and build the authority of your brand, and that is to become media. You can do that by hosting your own podcast. They are wildly successful and considered "new" media. I have hosted my podcast talk show, now incorporating multiple live streams, since 2008. It has allowed me to continue to build my authority and interview some cool people. Listen in at Sharvette.com.

When we think about and talk about written intellectual property, how do we showcase our intellectual property in writing? One of the things that may be missed these days is a blog. I highly encourage and highly recommend that entrepreneurs have a blog on their main website.

What is a blog? A blog features articles, tips, and short stories. What is a benefit of a blog? Google is looking for articles. For example, when someone goes to search on Google and let's say they put in the word *leadership,* Google is looking for articles on leadership. Google will also show videos or podcasts related to the topic.

So as an authority figure and increasing your authority, you want to have some intellectual property that's written on your platform that Google and any of the other search engines can search and recommend to people. This can drive traffic to your website, which will increase leads and sales. It also gives you fresh content for your website. Most search engines don't like stale content, which is a website that has not been updated or had anything new added in a while. I recommend adding a new blog one to four times per month.

Now, the last and biggest feature of establishing authority is to write a book or be a co-author in a book. Take a few seconds and look at the word *authority*. What is the root word of *authority*? Yes, you got it right…*author*.

It might be time for you to document your intellectual property or your transformational story into a book. Again, this can be done by writing a book yourself, or you can join forces and collaborate with other authors to create a book collaboration or anthology. For instance, books like the famous *Chicken Soup for the Soul* series are collaborations.

You can publish a book through the self-publishing option or certainly you can work with a publisher or shop your book to a major publishing house. When you write a book, that gives a credibility stamp on your brand and on your business. To the average person, this proves and showcases that you are an authority in your field. It's also a door opener for speaking engagements, media exposure, and things of that nature because they often look for authors when they want to feature someone in media or at a speaking event.

For those who provide just services, we can't leave out that a book is actually a product, so it gives you a physical product to sell.

I know I've covered a lot in this chapter, and that's why I spend twelve months working with female entrepreneurs on these marketing, positioning, visibility, and authority activities. If you would like to learn more about The Platform Builder, please go to platformbuilder.biz.

Sharvette Mitchell

Sharvette Mitchell, referred to as The Platform Builder, works with small businesses to enable them to build their online platform so that they generate more revenue with an amazing personal brand. She does this in a couple of ways: by focusing on their visibility, marketing, and branding through one-on-one consulting, group coaching programs, speaking, and events.

Sharvette is a graduate of Virginia Commonwealth University with a bachelor of science in marketing. She brings to the table twenty-five years past experience in corporate America in the field of training and development and consumer compliance for a global bank.

Sharvette has been featured in publications such as *Huffington Post, AARP, Hope for Women* magazine, *The CEO Magazine, Rescue A CEO* blog and *SistaSense* magazine. Sharvette has also been seen on CBS 6 Monday Motivation, CBS 6 Virginia This Morning, The CW network, and Comcast cable.

In addition, she is an ICF professional certified leadership coach, a past member of the board of directors of James River Writers, and a former recipient of the *ACHI Magazine*'s Radio Personality of the Year award.

For more than fourteen years, she has hosted a weekly talk radio show, *The Sharvette Mitchell Radio Show,* which airs on Blog Talk Radio, Apple Podcast, iHeart Radio, and on her five live-streaming platforms. Lastly, Sharvette is the visionary author of four book collaborations, *Propel, Pour, Pursue,* and *Pearls.*

Find out more about Sharvette at Mitchell-Productions.com.

CPSIA information can be obtained
at www.ICGtesting.com
Printed in the USA
LVHW081559011022
729743LV00016B/869